THE MEASURE OF A
FAMILY

GENE A. GETZ

A Division of G/L Publications
Glendale, California, U.S.A.

Other good Regal reading by Gene A. Getz
The Measure of a Man
The Measure of a Church
The Measure of a Woman
Moses: Moments of Glory, Feet of Clay
Abraham: Trials and Triumphs

The foreign language publishing of all Regal books is under the direction of *Gospel Liter-ature International* (GLINT), a missionary assistance organization founded in 1961 by Dr. Henrietta C. Mears. Each year *Gospel Literature International* provides financial and techni-cal help for the adaptation, translation and publishing of books and Bible study materials in more than 85 languages for millions of people worldwide.

For more information you are invited to write *Gospel Literature International*, Glendale, California 91204.

Unless otherwise noted, Scripture quotations
are from the following versions:
Old Testament: *The New American Standard Bible*
© The Lockman Foundation 1960, 1962, 1963, 1968, 1971.
Used by permission.
New Testament: *The New International Version*. Copyright
© 1973 by the New York Bible Society International.
Used by permission.

Fifth Printing, 1979

Published by
Regal Books Division, G/L Publications
Glendale, California 91209
Printed in U.S.A.

Library of Congress Catalog Card No. 76-46872
ISBN 0-8307-0445-0

This book is affectionately dedicated
to my wife, Elaine,
and our three children—Renee, Robyn, and Kenton.
All of them have enriched my life immeasurably.
Without them, this volume
would never have become a reality.

CONTENTS

I would like to express special gratitude to my brothers and sisters in Christ who attend Fellowship Bible Church and its various branch churches in Dallas, Texas, all of whom I consider a part of my "larger family." I deeply appreciate their positive witness to the concepts in this book.

And thanks, too, to Dr. Harold Hoehner, Director of Doctoral Studies at Dallas Theological Seminary and Associate Professor of New Testament Literature and Exegesis. Dr. Hoehner first read this manuscript and offered some very helpful suggestions.

LOOKING FORWARD

The Bible is an unusual book. Unlike others, it seldom gives extensive descriptions of forms and patterns. Rather, it emphasizes functions and principles. This is unique. Most other books describe both. And this is understandable, for wherever you have people, you have function; and wherever you have function, you have form. In other words, you cannot have function without form; you cannot have organism without organization. But the Bible, in the most part, does not describe in detail the various forms that biblical functions took—particularly in the New Testament. In fact, biblical writers more frequently referred to functions without mentioning form at all.

This is especially true of the Church. Again and again, the functions of a local body of Christ are described. In New Testament days they engaged in a variety of functions—teaching, preaching, sharing, praising, singing, helping, and encouraging. But seldom are we told what forms these functions took. We know there *was* form—for you cannot have function without form. But since it is possible to describe function without describing form, biblical writers did it consistently.

This is one of the unusual aspects of Scripture. Forms and structures are basically cultural, whereas numerous biblical functions are supracultural. This is one important reason why Christianity has thrived in almost every country of the world. Most other major world religions so confuse form and function that it's virtually impossible for their system of beliefs to survive out of their cultures.

But Christianity is different. The few forms that are mentioned in the New Testament are merely means to achieve divine ends, whereas most biblical functions are absolute and essential. If God had specifically described the forms all biblical functions took, to this day people in the twentieth century would be trying to copy New Testament forms. In fact, some people desperately try to copy the few forms that *are* in the New Testament. Still others superimpose upon biblical texts forms that aren't even there.

God's plan, then, is that every church, no matter where it is located and no matter where it exists in history, always be New Testament *in function*. But to be truly New Testament, Christians must be free to develop creative forms and patterns—at any given time and in any given culture or subculture. This God-ordained freedom is one reason why Christianity has survived for nearly 2,000 years.

The same is true of the family. God describes biblical functions for various members of the family, but generally sets us free to develop the forms and structures necessary to truly be a New Testament family in the twentieth century and under all kinds of cultural conditions.

This is what this book is all about. The first eleven chapters describe basic biblical goals and functions for various family members living in a variety of situations. It also sets forth spiritual principles to guide the family in reaching these goals and carrying out these functions—no matter what the cultural circumstances. The final chapter gives basic suggestions regarding moving from function to form. Practical projects are also included at the end of each chapter to help you apply these biblical principles—wherever you are living and whatever your particular problems.

As you read, keep this important truth in mind: biblical goals, functions, and principles—*not* forms and patterns—represent God's divine standard for measuring a family unit. It is only as we evaluate ourselves in the light of biblical—*not* cultural—criteria that we can truly build a New Testament home.

Gene A. Getz

1 THE HOME
THE CHURCH IN MINIATURE

Though the Bible on occasions speaks pointedly about the home, it says relatively little when compared with what it teaches about the Church—the larger family of God. What it does say about the family is brief! For example, when Paul wrote to the Colossian Christians, he made four succinct statements in four short verses:

3:18—Wives, submit to your husbands, as is fitting in the Lord.

3:19—Husbands, love your wives and do not be harsh with them.

3:20—Children, obey your parents in everything, for this pleases the Lord.

3:21—Fathers, do not embitter your children, or they will become discouraged.

Only four verses out of 95 in this whole epistle are

devoted specifically to the home. In the Ephesian letter, though Paul elaborates on these same statements he made to the Colossians, only 16 verses out of 155 are devoted especially to the family (see Eph. 5:22—6:4).

Why, in the New Testament, is there so little emphasis on the family? Didn't Paul and the other writers believe in the importance of the home? Didn't they understand that the home is God's first institution?

These questions appear even more puzzling when you look at the remainder of the New Testament correspondence. Six of Paul's letters (Romans, 2 Corinthians, Galatians, Philippians, 1 Thessalonians, 2 Thessalonians) make no direct reference to the family whatsoever! (Paul does use an illustration from the home in 1 Thess. 2:7-11.) Only four of his other letters contain brief remarks. In 1 Corinthians he deals with several marriage problems. He refers to the care of widows in 1 Timothy, reflects on Timothy's home life in the second letter, and in his correspondence with Titus, he exhorts wives and mothers regarding proper behavior in the home.

The writer of Hebrews also says nothing about the family, nor do James and Jude. The apostle John makes no specific mention of the family in his three epistles, nor in the book of Revelation. The only other significant passage in the New Testament epistles specifically treating the family appears in Peter's first epistle, though he says nothing in his second letter.

Again, we must ask *why*. Since so many problems in the world—from time immemorial—originate in the home, why hasn't God given us a guidebook for the home? Why aren't larger portions of the New Testament devoted to this important institution? Why hasn't the Lord left us with more direct information and instructions?

The fact is, He has! You see, if we interpret the lack of references to the family per se as elevating the Church above the home in importance, we miss the significant fact that the Christian home in the New Testament world was almost synonymous with the Church. In reality, an individual household in some instances *was* a local church—at least in its initial days (see 1 Cor. 16:15). The home, particularly after Christians were banned from worshiping in the synagogues, became the primary place for them to meet together to worship God. Eventually they were able to build church buildings, but in the early days of the Church it was forbidden by law. Therefore, we discover numerous references in the New Testament to "household churches" (see Rom. 16:3-5; 1 Cor. 16:19; Col. 4:15; Philem. 2).

These observations lead us to a very important conclusion. What was written to the Church was also written to individual families. Most of the New Testament, then, can be applied directly to individual family units. We *do* have a guidebook for the family unit! The Church simply becomes an umbrella concept that includes the home. The family is really the *Church in miniature.* True, on occasions the New Testament writers zero in on special needs that are uniquely related to family living. But in the most part, what was written to believers as a whole applies directly to Christian living in the smaller context of the home.

13

The Marks of a Mature Family

What Paul and other writers of the Scripture classified as the most important marks of a mature Church stand out clearly on the pages of the New Testament. When they wrote to a church they were proud of, they frequently thanked God for corporate *faith*, corporate *hope*, and corporate *love*—but especially for *love* (see Col. 1:3,4; 1 Thess. 1:2,3). When they wrote to a church that needed to develop one or more of these qualities, they encouraged that development (see Eph. 1:15,18; 2 Thess. 1:3,4). Thus Paul wrote to the Corinthians, a very immature and carnal church: "And now these three remain: faith, hope, and love. But the greatest of these is love. Follow the way of love" (1 Cor. 13:13; 14:1).[1]

Since the family in the New Testament is in reality the Church in miniature, it follows naturally that the maturity level of a Christian family can also be determined by the degree of faith, hope, and love expressed by that family as a whole—particularly on the part of dad, mom, and older children. Small children who are constantly exposed to this kind of life-style will usually begin to imitate the same qualities in their lives. But this development comes primarily through example, not by exhortations. Under normal conditions, our children will eventually become what we are!

How do we recognize these qualities in ourselves—and in our children? *Faith* is the capacity to believe God; to trust Him under all circumstances and in all situations; to remain faithful in good times and in bad; to not doubt His love and concern; to "hang on" to God when tragedy strikes, when confusion reigns, and when all else fails. "Faith is being sure of what we hope for and certain of what we do not see" (Heb. 11:1).

Hope is closely aligned with faith. However, it relates more specifically *to our eternal destiny*. It reflects steadfastness, doctrinal stability, and unwavering faith in the fact that Jesus Christ is coming again. It is recognized to the degree that family members demonstrate their hope of eternal life, their assurance of eternal salvation.

Love, succinctly defined, is Christlikeness. It includes all of those manifestations that characterize the Lord Jesus—particularly when He walked among men. "Love is patient, love is kind. It does not envy, it does not boast, it is not proud. It is not rude, it is not self-seeking, it is not easily angered, it keeps no record of wrongs. Love does not delight in evil but rejoices in the truth. It always protects, always trusts, always hopes, always perseveres. Love never fails" (1 Cor. 13:4-8).

Faith, hope, and love! These, then, are the marks of a mature church—*and* of a mature family. The New Testament writers made little distinction between church and home when they wrote letters to groups of New Testament believers.

Philemon—a Biblical Example of Maturity

One of the most striking illustrations of a mature household in the New Testament appears in one of Paul's very short letters. In our Bible it is only one chapter in length. From prison in Rome, he directed a letter to Philemon, a man who lived in Colossae and whom he called a "dear friend and fellow worker" (v.

1). Interestingly, he also addressed his greetings "to the church that meets in your [Philemon's] home" (v. 2).

Following Paul's salutation, he thanked God specifically for Philemon's maturity, a familiar pattern in Paul's letters. Notice the content of Paul's thanksgiving and prayer—"I always thank my God as I remember you in my prayers, because I hear about your *love* and *faith* in the Lord Jesus and your *love* for all the saints. I pray that you may be active in sharing your faith, so that you will have a full understanding of every good thing we have in Christ. Your love has given me great joy and encouragement, because you, brother, have refreshed the hearts of the saints"[2] (vv. 4-7).

Here we see the qualities of faith, hope, and love reflected in Philemon's life (hope is implied, though it is not mentioned specifically). As the head of his household, as a loving husband and sensitive father, his Christlike example influenced the total family unit. It always will. The father particularly represents the "God-image" in the home. And in New Testament days, correspondence directed to the head of a household was synonymous with directing it to the whole family. Paul was, in reality, thanking God for the maturity level of Philemon's whole household.

The rest of Paul's letter develops an intriguing story. Paul appealed to Philemon—"on the basis of love" (v. 9)—for a young man named Onesimus, who had been one of Philemon's slaves. It appears that when Philemon became a Christian he took Paul's instructions seriously to treat his slaves no longer as dirt under his pagan feet, but as fellow human beings, as fellow believers, as brothers and sisters in Jesus Christ (see Eph. 6:5-9; Col. 3:22—4:1). But Onesimus was a rebellious and irresponsible young man, and evidently did not respond to the gospel of Christ. He took advantage of his new freedom and new relationship with his master and escaped from Philemon's household, no doubt taking with him stolen goods.

In the providence of God, Onesimus ended up in Rome and came in contact with Paul who was in prison. There the apostle led him to a personal relationship with Jesus Christ and taught him the Word of God. Onesimus responded to Paul's loving exhortations. In fact, a great Christian relationship developed between this old apostle and the young slave boy.

Onesimus became a great source of encouragement as he ministered to Paul's personal needs. And in his humanness, Paul wanted Onesimus to stay with him in Rome. But eventually, though it was emotionally painful, he confronted the young man with his responsibility to his real master. And then Paul wrote a letter to Philemon—to build a bridge between Onesimus and Philemon. "I appeal to you," wrote Paul, "for my son Onesimus, who became my son while I was in chains. Formerly he was useless to you, but now he has become useful both to you and to me. I am sending him—who is my very heart—back to you" (vv. 10-12).

In spite of Paul's emotional involvement with Onesimus, his sincere but forceful logic with Philemon flowed from his pen with pointed accuracy. His target? Philemon's heart of love—his Christian

17

maturity—and Paul did not miss the mark. As we'll see, only a Christian friend with pure motives could approach Philemon as did Paul. Such an approach could only be taken with a mature man of God—a man of faith, hope, and love—a man like Philemon.

Friendship. First, he appealed to Philemon by elevating Onesimus to Philemon's own level. You see, Philemon was one of Paul's greatest and closest friends. To raise a useless slave to Philemon's level was to demonstrate to this man how much Onesimus' life had changed by his encounter with Jesus Christ. Thus he wrote: "I would have liked to keep him with me so that he could take your place in helping me while I am in chains for the gospel" (v. 13).

Courtesy. He next appealed to Philemon through courtesy, by respecting him as the kind master and owner of Onesimus. Though he knew in his heart that Philemon would have approved of Onesimus staying in Rome, Paul did not want to take his friend for granted. Hence, Paul wrote: "But I did not want to do anything without your consent, so that any favor you do will be spontaneous and not forced" (v. 14).

Providence. Next, Paul appealed to Philemon on the basis of the principle of Romans 8:28—God's providential work in the lives of Christians: "Perhaps the reason he was separated from you for a little while was that you might have him back for good—no longer as a slave, but better than a slave, as a dear brother" (vv. 15,16).

Equality. Paul next drives home a point that must have amazed Philemon. He raised Onesimus to his own level of relationship with Philemon—demonstrating Paul's view that *all* people, no matter what

18

their status in life, are *one* in Christ Jesus: "He is very dear to me but even dearer to you, both as a man and as a brother in the Lord. So if you consider me a partner, welcome him as you would welcome me" (vv. 16,17).

Personal responsibility. Paul's sincere but devastating psychology with his rich friend reached its zenith in his next statement. He took full responsibility for Onesimus' previous behavior. "If he has done you any wrong or owes you anything, charge it to me. I, Paul, am writing this with my own hand. I will pay it back—not to mention that you owe me your very self. I do wish, brother, that I may have some benefit from you in the Lord; refresh my heart in Christ" (vv. 18-20).

Confidence. Paul's final appeal culminated with a positive statement as to what he believed Philemon would actually do: "Confident of your obedience, I write to you, knowing that you will do even more than I ask" (v. 21). By this time, of course, Philemon could do no less. Paul had made his point.

This story, probably more than any other in the New Testament, gives us tremendous insight into Philemon's family life. First, he served as a dynamic Christlike example to his whole household. Though a man of wealth, he became a man of faith, of hope, and of Christlike love. He had no doubt led his whole family and household to Christ—including his slaves. He had created a new environment for everyone. His attitudes toward everyone demonstrated love and concern and he also treated his slaves as brothers and sisters in Christ. He became a man of hospitality, inviting the church to meet in his home and using it as a place for traveling missionaries to stay. Thus Paul could write in total freedom, as he closed his letter— "Prepare a guest room for me, because I hope to be restored to you in answer to your prayers" (v. 22).

Developing a New Testament Home

Every Christian home in the New Testament world was to function as a Church in miniature. In fact, some households in themselves *were* local churches. And the marks of maturity for both home and church were faith, hope, and love. Whatever was written to local churches was in essence written to individual family units. Therefore, the whole of the New Testament, and particularly the New Testament correspondence, serves as a guideline for family living.

But what about the marks of Christian maturity? How does your family—my family—measure up? We often speak today of having a "New Testament church," but do we also think about having a "New Testament home"?

1. What about faith? When have your children really observed your faith? Test yourselves! What is the first thing you do when you face a crisis? Do you complain, murmur, fall apart, strike out at others (or even at God)? Do you get nervous, upset, frustrated? Do you worry, fret, stew? Or do you first turn your eyes heavenward and pray? Do you demonstrate a sense of trust in God, that He is in control, and that all things *can* work together for good to those who love the Lord (see Rom. 8:28)? Furthermore, do you deliberately and prayerfully take action, using God's principles to guide you? You see, your children observe these actions—positive or negative. What are they learning?

Furthermore, when have your children participated with you as parents in a venture in faith? Have you ever done anything together that really tests your faith?

Warning: Make sure you are not naive at this point. For example, it's usually not very wise to buy a child a bicycle with money you don't have, hoping it will be supplied. You may be teaching him irresponsibility rather than faith. However, what about trusting God together to help you reach your neighbors for Christ? How about trusting God to change someone's attitude or viewpoint—a teacher, a coach, a friend?

Note: Be ready to participate in God's answer. Sometimes we pray, and God answers by giving us an open door to participate in the solution and to bring the answer to fulfillment. But often we miss the opportunity. For example, God may help build a bridge to a neighbor but we may fail to walk across the bridge. This, of course, becomes faith without works —which the Bible says is dead!

Big question: What are your children (and neighbors) learning about *faith* from your life-style?

2. *What about hope?* As parents, how secure are you in Jesus Christ? Do you *know* you have eternal life through faith in Jesus Christ? What is the primary focus of your life—this world or the world to come? How do you view the second coming of Jesus Christ? Do you live day by day in the light of His return? And what is your attitude toward those who don't know Jesus Christ? Do you view them as people "without

hope"? Are you concerned about them? Do you share your faith with others?

Big question: What are your children (and neighbors) learning about *hope* from your life-style?

3. *What about love?* How specifically do you show your love for God? As husband and wife, how loving are you toward each other? And how loving are you toward your children? What are others learning from you about Christlikeness, about patience, about kindness, humility, concern, sensitivity, unselfishness, even temper, forgiveness, and pure motives? Are they learning what love really is?

Big question: What are your children (and neighbors) learning about *love* from your life-style?

God's ideal is that the man of the house, the husband and father, should be primarily responsible for leading his family, for setting the tone for spiritual and psychological development. His example, like Philemon's, is basic to effective Christian communication in the family. His attitudes set the stage for creating unity and oneness. As he develops the quality of hospitality, his home will become a place where others feel welcome.

In cases where the husband and father may be a non-Christian (as in Timothy's home), the mother will need to take the primary responsibility for exemplifying Jesus Christ to her children *and* to her unsaved husband. And as we'll see in future chapters, the Bible gives some unique guidelines for unique situations.

Note: Not all non-Christian husbands and fathers are *bad* husbands and fathers. Some, in fact, do a better job of providing and loving than some carnal

Christians. So be careful how you judge. Becoming a Christian doesn't automatically make you a successful leader in your home.

Life Response

Consider the *big questions!* How would you evaluate your role as a parent? How would you evaluate your corporate maturity as a family? And what can you do immediately to measure up more effectively to God's criteria?

Family or Group Project

Step 1: Review the material in this chapter. Then as individual members of your group or family, select an area where you need to improve the most. Is it faith, hope, or love? You may wish to have each family or group member make this decision in the quietness of his own heart.

Step 2: Discuss as a family how you can more effectively manifest one of these qualities corporately, that is, as a family unit.

Footnotes
1. See *The Measure of a Church* by Gene A. Getz, published by Regal Publications, for an in-depth treatment of these three concepts.
2. Italics added. Hereafter all italics in Scripture quotations are added by the author.

2 THE HOME
ITS CHRISTIAN DISTINCTIVES

What made the Christian family a unique social unit in the New Testament world? How did Christian homes compare with pagan families?

The World in Miniature

Though secular history records that various family life-styles were in vogue in New Testament times, the Bible stands as the best source of information. The world situation in general represented family life in particular. As a Christian family was to function as the "Church in miniature," so the non-Christian family represented the "world in miniature." In other words, just as the maturity level of a local church reflected the maturity level of individual family units (and vice versa), so the morality level of the world system reflected the morality level of the families

25

that made up that world (and again, vice versa).

What, then, was the universal situation? What characterized the pagan community, and consequently its family units? Paul answered these questions clearly when he wrote to the Ephesian Christians: "So I tell you this, and insist on it in the Lord, that you must no longer live as the Gentiles do, in the futility of their thinking. They are darkened in their understanding and separated from the life of God because of the ignorance that is in them due to the hardening of their hearts. Having lost all sensitivity, they have given themselves over to sensuality so as to indulge in every kind of impurity, with a continual lust for more" (Eph. 4:17-19).

This passage represents Paul's description of the Gentiles' life-style. These people were darkened, separated, ignorant, and hardened. Their lives were characterized by futility, insensitivity, sensuality, and impurity.

Paul also pointedly described New Testament world conditions in his first letter to Timothy, who at that time was also in Ephesus. True, he was speaking of the last days, but at that time Paul had no way of knowing he was not living in the final days before Jesus Christ's return. God did not reveal to Paul His eschatological timetable. Consequently, his writings reflect that he always lived in the light of Christ's second coming.

Only toward the end of his life did Paul appear to realize that he would probably die before Jesus Christ came again. But even then he felt it would only be a matter of time after his departure before Christ would return. Notice what he said about world conditions in his final letter before his own death: "But mark this: There will be terrible times in the last days. People will be lovers of themselves, lovers of money, boastful, proud, abusive, *disobedient to their parents*, ungrateful, unholy, without love, unforgiving, slandering, without self-control, brutal, not lovers of the good, treacherous, rash, conceited, lovers of pleasure rather than lovers of God—having a form of godliness but denying its power" (2 Tim. 3:1-5).

Though all of these characteristics no doubt reflected the conditions in many pagan families at that time, one, of course, stands out in bold relief—children were "disobedient to their parents." They had little, if any, respect and honor for the ones who had brought them into the world. As we'll see in a later chapter, when Paul used the word "children," he was, in the most part, not referring to *little* children. Rather he was talking about grown, mature children, children who know better.

General Guidelines for the Family

In the light of the conditions that existed in the average non-Christian family, what was to be true of the Christian family that lived in the midst of the pagan world? Again, Paul, in his letter to the Ephesians, answered this question in several very descriptive paragraphs. For what were guidelines for the Church, were also guidelines for the family.

After describing the Gentile world, Paul said: "You, however, did not come to know Christ that way. Surely you heard of him and were taught in him in accordance with the truth that is in Jesus. You were taught, with regard to your former way of life, to *put off your old self*, which is being corrupted by its deceitful desires; to be made new in the attitude of your minds; and to *put on the new self*, created to be like God in true righteousness and holiness" (Eph. 4:20-24).

Following this graphic description of a Christian's new position in Christ, the apostle then went on to detail some specific actions which should no longer be practiced by followers of Jesus Christ in the home, in the Church, or as they rubbed shoulders with their pagan friends. His list implies that believers *should* practice the traits opposite to those they are to put off.

Honesty: "Each of you must put off falsehood and speak truthfully to his neighbor" (Eph. 4:25).

Self-control: "In your anger do not sin: Do not let the sun go down while you are still angry" (4:26).

Integrity: "He who has been stealing must steal no longer" (4:28).

Diligence: He "must work, doing something useful with his own hands" (4:28).

Unselfishness: His goal should be to "have something to share with those in need" (4:28).

Discretion: "Do not let any unwholesome talk come out of your mouths" (4:29).

Concern: Speak only "what is helpful for building others up" (4:29).

Sensitivity to God: "Do not grieve the Holy Spirit of God" (4:30).

Following these specific exhortations, Paul summarized his thoughts and put it all together: "Get rid of all bitterness, rage, and anger, brawling and slander, along with every form of malice. Be kind and compassionate to one another, forgiving each other, just as in Christ God forgave you. Be imitators of God, therefore, as dearly loved children, and *live a life of love*, just as Christ loved us and gave himself up for us as a fragrant offering and sacrifice to God" (4:31—5:2).

Special Guidelines for the Family

Though Paul's instructions to the Church are also instructions to the family, he had some special things to say to family members in particular. Thus when Paul was writing his letter to the Ephesian believers about Christian living in general, he succinctly high-lighted those characteristics that should *especially* set the Christian family off from the typical pagan family. In doing so, he dealt with four significant relationships that are similar to relationships in the Church, but are also uniquely different:

Wives to husbands: "Wives, submit to your husbands as to the Lord" (5:22).

Husbands to wives: "Husbands, love your wives, just as Christ loved the church" (5:25).

Children to parents: "Children, obey your parents in the Lord" (6:1).

Fathers to children: "Fathers, do not exasperate your children; instead, bring them up in the training and instruction of the Lord" (6:4).

To understand clearly what Paul was saying, it is important to note the total context of these statements, both scripturally and culturally. Frequently, we discuss the words "submission," "love," and "obedience" in isolation, which leads to extreme viewpoints—particularly as it relates to the place and position of women and children in the home.

Let me explain what I mean. The words "submission," "love," "obedience," and "honor," and the concept of "nurture with patience" are not used exclusively and respectively with "wives," "husbands," "children," and "fathers." Rather, these words are used to describe relationships among *all* members of the body of Christ. *All* Christians are to "submit to one another" (5:21)—which means husbands to wives as well as wives to husbands. *All* Christians are to "live a life of love" (5:2). *All* Christians are to obey and honor those who are in positions of authority (see Heb. 13:17; 1 Thess. 5:12,13). And those in authority in the church are not to lord it over those who have been entrusted to them, but rather are to be "examples to the flock" (1 Pet. 5:3). Furthermore, we are *all* to avoid discouraging each other and we're *all* to teach and admonish one another (see Heb. 3:13; Col. 3:16).

In other words, since the home is the Church in miniature, this means that husbands are also to *submit* to their wives, wives are to *love* their husbands, children are to *love* and *submit* to their parents, and both parents are to be *sensitive* to their children.

This leads us, however, to a very interesting question. If these words can be used to describe *all* relationships in the family, why then does Paul single out these concepts to specifically describe *certain* relationships in the home? A careful look at the New Testament culture and at the total context of Scripture reveals at least two basic reasons. First, there was a need to emphasize these functions at this time because of the cultural conditions and pressures in the

New Testament world. This we'll describe in more detail in future chapters.

Second, in God's plan for the family, these functions take on particular significance, and there are at least two reasons why this is true.

I must warn you! When you read the next two sections some of you will want to throw this book away—especially those of you who may be strong for women's rights. But I assure you that I am for women's rights, too. I'd like to ask you to hear me out. Then if you still think I'm wrong from a biblical and psychological perspective, let me know. I try hard to be teachable.

1. Theological reasons. Since creation, God has established certain specific roles for the family members. God created man first, thus placing upon his shoulders greater responsibility for the affairs of the home. And it follows naturally that woman is to recognize this God-ordained responsibility. Thus Paul reminds the Christian women in Ephesus that "the husband is the head of the wife as Christ is the head of the church" (5:23).

Likewise, God gave parents authority over children. He made it very clear in the Ten Commandments that children are to honor their fathers and mothers. But on the other hand, this gave fathers no right to dominate and control their children in such a way so as to destroy their individuality.

2. Psychological reasons. Inherent in God's ordained functions for husbands and wives, and parents and children, are also psychological laws. God's theological statements, when interpreted correctly, will normally work in harmony with the psychological nature of man. When these theological and psychological laws are violated, man cannot reach his complete potential in terms of inner security and happiness. Thus what Paul says to family members is for our benefit. As much as is possible, he wants us to be fulfilled people.

Human beings, then who work against God's laws will never find what they are looking for, no matter how sincere their efforts. It is ironic, of course, that some groups who talk most about fulfillment will never find it apart from bringing their lives into conformity with God's ordained will. There is no other way. We can shake our fist at God, call Him a "she," and even deny His existence. But it does not change reality. God *does* exist. He has established certain roles for family members, and if we violate them we will not find true happiness. Our present frustrations and anxieties will only be accentuated and will eventually turn to bitterness and disillusionment.

God Has a Unique Plan for the Family

But there is an even more significant reason why God has established specific roles for Christian family members, and why He, through His servant Paul, emphasized them in the Ephesian and Colossian letters. It has to do with *why* we are in the world. Let me put it in total perspective:

Why did Paul say, "Wives, submit to your husbands as to the Lord"?

First, it is God's ordained plan that a woman should not dominate or control her husband. And the opposite was becoming a trend in the pagan world, particularly in the vicinity of Ephesus.

32

Second, submitting is one of the most difficult things for many wives to do. Ever since sin entered the world it is a natural tendency for *all* human beings to resist authority. In fact, sin entered the world due to disobedience and an unwillingness to submit to God's authority. Thus Paul is treating a universal problem.

Third, when women violate this psychological law they will inevitably experience increased unhappiness and insecurity. On the other hand, when a woman conforms to this law, it produces the best results for her personally, it ministers in a significant way to her husband, and it creates special benefits for the family.

Fourth, and most important, when a woman does fulfill her God-ordained role, she is helping create an environment that will contribute significantly to *helping her family become an outstanding testimony to the non-Christian world*. In short, she is helping to carry out the Great Commission.

Why did Paul say, "Husbands, love your wives, just as Christ loved the church"?

First, it is God's ordained plan for a man to be a Christlike leader in the home.

Second, to love as Christ loved is the most difficult thing for a man to do, especially in a culture where women were often treated like slaves. Thus Paul emphasized this in the Ephesian and Colossian letters.

Third, when a man loves as Christ loved, it produces the best results in his own life, in his wife's life, and in the life of his family.

Fourth, and again most important, when a man sets the example of loving his wife as Christ loved, it will permeate the whole family, creating unity and harmony, which in turn becomes the most basic ingredient *in being a witness to the non-Christian world.*

Why did Paul say, "Children, obey your parents in the Lord, for this is right. 'Honor your father and mother' "?

First, it is God's ordained plan.

Second, to have obedience and respect for parents is one of the most difficult things for children to do, especially in an environment where the trend is toward disobedience and dishonor, as it was in the New Testament world (and as it is in today's world).

Third, obedience and honor bring the best results in the lives of children and parents. It is a basic ingredient in creating harmony and happiness.

Fourth, and most important, homes where children obey and honor their parents become outstanding examples in the community and *bear an unusual testimony for Jesus Christ.*

Why did Paul say, "Fathers, do not exasperate your children; instead, bring them up in the training and instruction of the Lord"?

First, it is God's ordained plan (sound familiar?).

Second, the most difficult thing for men to do is to develop sensitivity toward their children and to begin to fulfill their God-ordained role of being responsible for their children's nurture. This was particularly true in the New Testament world (and also today). It was not a natural part of their life-style when they were converted. Women were basically responsible for the children while men spent most of their time "doing their own thing" and meeting their ego needs outside of the home.

Third, when a man fulfills this God-ordained role as a father to his children, it creates the best results in every member of the family—including his own personal happiness.

Fourth, and most important, when a father truly functions as a *caring* father, the impact upon the world is obvious. It actually sets the stage for *teaching non-Christian neighbors about God, the heavenly Father, who desires that all men come to know His Son, Jesus Christ.*

The Bridge to the World

From the perspective of space and time, God's ultimate purpose for every local church is to reveal the glory of God to all men and proclaim the message of Jesus Christ as the Saviour of the world. And since every family in the church represents the "Church in miniature," it also follows that God's ultimate purpose for every family unit is the same as His purpose for the Church.

God's great plan for all believers involves living in the world as local bodies of believers who love each other dearly and who demonstrate a unity and oneness of heart and spirit that in turn conveys to the world that Christ truly came from God. This is obvious from Christ's prayer for His disciples in John 17: "My prayer is not for them alone. I pray also for those who will believe in me through their message, that all of them may be one, Father, just as you are in me and I am in you. May they also be in us so that the world may believe that you have sent me. I have given them the glory that you gave me, that they may be one as we are one: I in them and you in me. May they be brought to complete *unity to let the world know* that you sent me and have loved them even as you have loved me" (John 17:20-23).

Since this is God's plan for every local church, it is also His plan that every family unit convey the same message to non-Christian neighbors. In fact, in most cultures the home can become the *primary* means for revealing love and unity. The home is a nonthreatening environment to which to invite non-Christians. A church building, on the other hand, often becomes a source of anxiety for people who are religious dropouts, or who have had a bad experience with Christians.

What factors cause a home to be a vibrant testimony to the community? This was, it seemed, the primary burden of Paul's emphasis in the Ephesian and Colossian letters. The factors are clear. A home becomes a dynamic testimony to the world when wives submit to their husbands as to the Lord; when husbands love their wives just as Christ loved the Church; when children respect, honor, and obey their parents in the Lord; and when fathers do not exasperate and discourage their children, but rather bring them up in the training and instruction of the Lord. This process in itself produces unity and oneness, and in turn, the unity and oneness form the dynamic bridge to non-Christian neighbors—a bridge over which we can walk to share the direct message of the gospel and to lead other families to Jesus Christ.

Life Response

Select the appropriate response for you, and make it your prayer:

☐ As a wife, I will evaluate my role, especially my attitude and behavior toward my husband. I will attempt to be totally Christian in all that I do, submitting to my husband as to the Lord.

☐ As a husband, I will evaluate my role, especially my attitudes and actions toward my wife. I want to be totally Christian in all that I do, loving as Christ loves. I will also do all I can to make submission a two-way street, without abdicating my role as head of my household.

☐ As a child or young person at home, I will evaluate my role, especially my attitude and behavior toward my parents. I will do all I can to respect, honor, and obey them.

☐ As a father, I will evaluate my role, especially my attitude and behavior toward my children. I will do all I can not to exasperate or discourage them, but rather to bring them up in the nurture and admonition of the Lord.

Family or Group Project

Discuss how you can, as a family, carry out the following commitment: "As a family we will do all we can to be a dynamic witness in our community, beginning by having each member of the family fulfill his or her God-ordained role."

3 THE CHRISTIAN WIFE
AND SUBMISSION

Paul's directive to wives to submit to their husbands, both in his Ephesian and Colossian letters, has probably become one of the most controversial statements in the whole Bible, particularly in the decade of the '70s. Most non-Christians deny the authority of the Scripture and brush aside Paul's statement as cultic and medieval. To them, it's one man's opinion —and a very prejudiced one at that. Sociologists and psychologists could find many reasons to classify Paul as maladjusted, neurotic, egocentric, or even bitter. And some modern-day "liberated women" might use stronger terms.

However, even some Christians who claim to believe in the full inspiration of the Bible have reinterpreted Paul's statement. Some say that there isn't such a thing as ordained authority, either in the family or in the church. Their key word is "egalitarianism." Pointing to Paul's statement in Galatians 3:28 that in Christ there is neither "male nor female," they try to demonstrate from Scripture that we are all one and totally equal in all respects.

Other Christians try to resolve this tension by pointing out that Paul was overly influenced by his religious upbringing. Thus he penned "God's Word" with subjective tendencies. The problem with this view, of course, is that it opens the door to error in Scripture, and if Paul made a mistake at this point, what about his view of "justification by faith"?

Still other Christians, unwilling to go this far, interpret Paul's statement as a non-absolute, reflecting cultural problems in the New Testament Church. Consequently, they do not feel Paul's statement is normative for today. He was merely dealing with a *particular problem* in a *particular church* at a *particular time* in history.

Granted, there are statements in the Bible that are strictly cultural. For example, Paul on several occasions instructed New Testament Christians to "greet all the brothers with a holy kiss" (see 1 Thess. 5:26; Rom. 16:16; 1 Cor. 16:20; 2 Cor. 13:12; 1 Pet. 5:14). That which is absolute in this statement is the fact that Christians are always to "greet one another in love," but the form or pattern of that greeting varies from culture to culture. In our culture, a kiss of greeting may not be acceptable, whereas in the New Testament culture it was common, as it is today in some cultures, even among non-Christians.

But is Paul's directive regarding submission in

Ephesians 5:22 and Colossians 3:18 in the same category? What *is* a biblical position on submission? What did Paul (and other writers of Scripture) really mean? To answer these questions we must look at the *whole* of Scripture, not at isolated texts. We must also beware of subjective interpretations, trying to make the Bible prove what we want to believe. If we do this, I'm confident we can arrive at God's true perspective on the husband-wife relationship.

Before and After the Fall

The concept of submission is not a truth propagated only by the apostle Paul. In fact, Paul's basic scriptural authority for his statements is rooted and grounded in the creation story. As you know, God first created man. But then He said: "It is not good for the man to be alone; I will make him a helper suitable for him" (Gen. 2:18).

And of course, God did! He "caused a deep sleep to fall upon the man, and he slept; then He took one of his ribs, and closed up the flesh at that place. And the Lord God fashioned into a woman the rib which He had taken from the man, and brought her *to the man*" (Gen. 2:21,22).

Many years later, when the apostle Paul was discussing the subject of worship with the Corinthian Christians, he argued a point based upon this same biblical truth from the creation story. Said he: "For man did not come from woman, but *woman from man;* neither was man created for woman, but *woman for man*" (1 Cor. 11:8,9).

Here Paul was referring to God's order in creation, and also to His purpose in creating woman. And what he is referring to happened before sin came into the world. In other words, woman's present relationship to man is affected not only by the fall, but by God's original plan when He created woman *for* man.

Paul makes this truth even stronger when he emphasizes that man is "the image and *glory of God;* but the woman is the *glory of man*" (1 Cor. 11:7). By creation man first reflected God's unique image. Since woman was taken from man, she, in a special way, reflected the unique image of man—although certainly it follows that she also reflected the image of God just as Adam did.

The apostle Peter affirms this same concept. Speaking primarily of women who were married to non-Christian husbands, he said without equivocation: "Wives, in the same way be *submissive* to your husbands" (1 Pet. 3:1). Later in the same passage he illustrated submission by referring to women in the Old Testament: "They were *submissive,*" said Peter, "to their own husbands, like Sarah, who obeyed Abraham and called him her master. You are her daughters if you do what is right and do not give way to fear" (1 Pet. 3:5,6).

It hardly seems feasible to interpret these passages explaining submission and divine order in both the Old and New Testaments as purely cultural statements. The whole tone of Scripture teaches that man, by creation, has a position of authority in the family. It is God's ordained plan—from the very beginning of creation.

But woman's relationship to man was also affected by the entrance of sin into the human race. After Eve, and then Adam, had disobeyed, God clearly referred to the effect of sin upon their relationship. To Eve, God said: "I will greatly multiply your pain in childbirth, in pain you shall bring forth children; yet your desire shall be for your husband, and he shall rule over you" (Gen. 3:16).

Woman's submissive role to man, then, *antedates the fall*, but was *complicated by the fall*. Once sin entered the human race, it set up all kinds of problems in the relationship between man and woman; one being that man, too, became a sinner, causing him to abuse and misuse his God-ordained role as head of the household. But more about this concept in the next chapter.

Submission in the Church

The principle of consistency is a very important concept when interpreting in the Scriptures what is cultural and what is supracultural; what is non-absolute and what is absolute. Another evidence that the concept of submission is not cultural is that Paul extends this idea to relationships between men and women in the Church. Here again we see the unique relationship between the Church and the home.

In the Corinthian assembly, women were obviously engaging in activities that were in violation of the principle of submission. Thus Paul wrote: "As in all the congregations of the saints, women should remain silent in the churches. They are not allowed to speak, but must *be in submission*, as the Law says" (1 Cor. 14:33,34).

When Paul wrote to Timothy, he stressed the same point: "A woman should learn in quietness and *full submission*. I do not permit a woman to teach or to have authority over a man; she must be silent" (1 Tim. 2:11,12). In this very passage Paul argues his point again from the *order of creation:* "For Adam was formed first, then Eve" (v. 13). He also argues his point from the standpoint of sin entering the human race: "And Adam was not the one deceived; it was the woman who was deceived and became a sinner" (1 Tim. 3:14). Adam, of course, also sinned, but Eve sinned first.

Thus we see consistency in scriptural teaching about the relationship between men and women. Whether in the home or in the Church, men were to be in a position of primary responsibility and authority.

What Does the Bible Mean by "Submission"?

There are many and varied interpretations of what the Bible teaches about women and the concept of submission. Most of these interpretations are based upon the passages we've just looked at. What is the Bible actually saying? It is helpful to discover what the Bible *is* teaching by also looking at what it *is not* teaching.

The Bible does not teach that women are the only ones who are to practice submission.

Paul in the very passage where he exhorted wives to submit to their husbands (see Eph. 5:22), also introduced this concept by exhorting all believers to "submit to one another out of reverence for Christ" (Eph. 5:21). This is to be the universal principle for *all* members of the body of Christ, including wives to husbands and husbands to wives. Paul extended this concept of mutual submission to the intimacies of marriage when he wrote to the Corinthians: "The husband should fulfill his marital duty to his wife, and likewise the wife to her husband. The wife's body does not belong to her alone but also to her husband. In the same way, the husband's body does not belong to him alone but also to his wife. Do not deprive each other except by mutual consent and for a time, so that you may devote yourselves to prayer. Then come together again so that Satan will not tempt you because of your lack of self-control" (1 Cor. 7:3-5).

The Bible does not teach that women should never, under any circumstances, say anything in the church.

In Paul's letter to the Colossians we see the functioning body and what *all* members of that body are to do for each other: "Let the word of Christ dwell in you richly as you *teach and counsel one another* with all wisdom, and as you sing psalms, hymns and spiritual songs with gratitude in your hearts" (Col. 3:16).

It is very clear in this passage that *all* members of the body of Christ—men and women—are to "teach and counsel one another." There are no exceptions in this passage. Is this not a contradiction with Paul's other statements that women are to be *silent* in the church?

The problem, it seems, is resolved when we see both "teaching" and "silence" as functions—functions that take on various *forms* and modes of expression or "non-expression." It is important to note that the Bible often defines function without describing form. But we must also remember that we cannot have function without form. Therefore, even though the Bible does not describe the "forms" that the women in Corinth and Ephesus were using, these forms were always present.

Evidently some women in these New Testament churches, especially in the Corinthian church, were using teaching and speaking forms in various ways to lord it over men and to create confusion in the body. They were usurping the place of leadership in the church. In doing so, they were violating God's principles of submission as it relates to women's special relationship to men. In fact, the forms they were using were creating so much confusion and disturbance and disorder that Paul warned them that unbelievers who came into the assembly would think they were out of their minds (1 Cor. 14:23).

When Paul dealt with this problem in Corinth and Ephesus, there is no doubt that the believers there knew exactly what Paul was talking about. They could interpret the word "silent" without any problem, whereas if we take the word literally to mean "no sound," it will lead us to logical absurdities.

But on the other hand, the concept of "not being in authority over men" is the supracultural principle that emerges from these passages of Scripture. In fact, it is possible for all members of the body of Christ, according to Paul's injunctions to the Colossians, to "teach and counsel one another," using forms that do not violate God's principle of submission, just as it is possible for men to submit to their wives without giving up their headship.

The Bible does not teach that women are second-class citizens.

Here is where Christianity, rightly interpreted, has elevated woman to a position unequalled in most other secular and religious societies and communities. First of all, the Bible teaches *total equality* in our relationship with God. Even Paul, who could very easily be classified as a male chauvinist if wrongly interpreted, stated without equivocation: "You are *all* sons of God through faith in Christ Jesus, for *all of you* who were united with Christ in baptism have been clothed with Christ. There is neither Jew nor Greek, slave nor free, *male nor female*, for you are all one in Christ Jesus" (Gal. 3:26-28).

Spiritually, then, God does not see differences between men and women. That's why Jesus said that there would be no marriages in heaven (see Mark 12:25). Sex distinctions will be nonexistent. And since God sees us in Christ at this very moment as if we were already glorified (see Rom. 8:30), we must certainly conclude that men and women are spiritually equal in God's sight.

On the other hand, the Bible recognizes that while on earth we are not yet glorified. We are still living in these bodies of clay in a world contaminated by sin. And every person who views men and women objectively must acknowledge certain distinctions between male and females that are more complex than the obvious differences in our reproductive physiology and external appearances.

The Bible recognizes this, too. In fact, in the same passage in which the apostle Peter reminds his readers that women are spiritual equals with men (he calls a Christian woman a "fellow-heir of the grace of life" [1 Pet. 3:7, *NASB*]), he also exhorts men to "treat them [women] with respect as the weaker partner" (1 Pet. 3:7).

Some women, of course, when they hear this statement, react emotionally. And understandably so. Down through history women generally have been misused and abused—even in so-called Christian communities. But here in this passage, Peter is stating a simple fact. By creation, women in some respects are not as strong as men. Physically, their frames have certain limitations. Though they are very capable of hard work in many areas, and certainly are not weaker intellectually, most women are not capable of playing professional football with men. There is a certain point beyond which most women cannot go, and by design—God's design. Thus Peter exhorts husbands: "In the same way be considerate as you live with your wives and treat them with respect as the weaker partner and as heirs with you in the gracious gift of life, so that nothing will hinder your prayers" (1 Pet. 3:7).

The Bible does not teach that women are incapable of great achievements.

This is obvious from history and our present culture. The world is filled with examples of great women whose achievements have even far exceeded those of many men. Some of our greatest artists, musicians, writers, scientists, administrators, and communicators are women.

Paul himself made several significant references to women who had evidently had unusual ministries in New Testament days. Even though he had to admonish Euodia and Syntyche regarding their personal differences and conflicts with each other, he also referred to the way they had assisted him in the ministry (see Phil. 4:2,3). And, of course, Aquila and

Priscilla stand out in the New Testament as a great husband and wife team who together ministered the Word of God (see Rom. 16:3,4; 1 Cor. 16:19).

But we must also conclude that one of woman's greatest achievements has been her contributions to man. In fact, it is more than just a cliché to say that "behind most great men stand great women."

In my own life—though I certainly would hesitate to classify my achievements as great—what I *have* achieved, to a great extent, I must attribute to my wife. There's no one like her who can encourage me when I'm discouraged; who can restore my self-image when it is shattered; who can bolster my spirit when I'm depressed; who can motivate me to keep on "keeping on" when the road of life gets rough.

This should not be surprising. In fact, it makes sense, because this is a basic reason why God created woman in the first place—to be a helper to man. No, the Bible does not say she was created to be his servant or his slave, but rather a helper—literally, a "helper as his counterpart." She was created to be his complement, and in many respects his equal. But yet she was to recognize man's authority in her life.

Paul expressed this unique balance in his first letter to the Corinthians. After stating explicitly that woman was created for man (see 1 Cor. 11:9), he hurriedly added: "In the Lord, however, woman is not independent of man, nor is man independent of woman. For as woman came from man, so also man is born of woman. But everything comes from God" (1 Cor. 11:11,12).

The Bible does not teach that women should never express their opinions and their feelings.

49

There are some Christian men who refuse to allow their wives to express their feelings and frustrations, their anxiety and anger. Any disagreement is put down with the "authority" of Scripture.

Nothing could be more biblically inaccurate or devastating to a woman's self-worth and emotional and spiritual health. This is a direct violation of Peter's exhortation to husbands to treat their wives "with respect" and "as heirs" in Christ Jesus. And it is also a direct violation of many biblical injunctions that exhort all Christians to "be devoted to one another" (Rom. 12:10), to "accept one another" (Rom. 15:7), to "serve one another" (Gal. 5:13), to "carry each other's burdens" (Gal 6:2), and to "encourage each other" (1 Thess. 4:18). Paul made it very clear in his Corinthian letter that all Christians are to have "equal concern for each other" (1 Cor. 12:25). And then he adds: "If one part suffers, every part suffers with it" (v. 26).

The Christian husband who is not sensitive to his wife, who does not listen to her complaints, who does not identify with her emotional and physical pain, is in direct violation of God's will. He is no doubt using the Scriptures to justify his own weak ego and his selfish egotistical behavior.

The Bible does not teach that a woman cannot be active outside the home, even pursuing a professional career.

Some Christians have a very narrow view of this issue, insisting that the "woman's place is in the home." Granted, the Bible teaches that, for a married woman, home is her primary place of responsibility. Meeting her husband's and children's needs should be a priority above everything else, except her personal relationship with God. And if she neglects these priorities in order to develop a professional career or to accumulate material wealth, she is violating the direct teachings of Scripture. Paul was very explicit about this issue. Older women, he said, should "train the younger women to love their husbands and children, to be self-controlled and pure, to be busy at home, to be kind, and to be subject to their husbands, so that no one will malign the word of God" (Titus 2:4,5).

On the other hand, to force a woman to be merely a homemaker is also to violate scriptural principles. There are some women who are quite capable of carrying out their biblical priorities, while doing many other things as well. Consider, for example, the "excellent wife" described in Proverbs 31. Among her many activities and accomplishments, "she considers a field and buys it," and "from her earnings she plants a vineyard . . . . She extends her hands to the poor; and she stretches out her hands to the needy" (Prov. 31:16,20).

The Bible does not teach that a woman must subject herself to physical and psychological abuse that is beyond her ability to bear.

Unfortunately, some women are married to men who are so self-centered and evil in their actions that it is impossible to cope with the problems they present. No matter what the wife does to try to be submissive, the husband only takes greater advantage. A man like this is sick—both spiritually and psychologically. At this point, the Christian wife needs to seek help and advice from the elders and pastors of the church. She cannot bear the problem alone (see Matt. 18:15-17; Jas. 5:13-16). In times like this, a woman needs help from other mature members of the body of Christ.

But a word of warning! Some women find it very easy to rationalize and project themselves as unappreciated martyrs, when in reality they have not been obedient to the Scriptures. They have defined submissiveness by their own standard—not by the Word of God. Here again mature members of the body of Christ can help a person develop objectivity about her problem. And if it is an absolutely unbearable situation, she may have to remove herself from it, but always with the hope that there will eventually be a change in her husband's attitudes and behavior.

What, then, does God mean when He says that wives are to submit to their husbands? In summary, to conform to God's will every woman must realize that the God of the universe has especially created woman for man. She was to be his helper, uniquely designed to complement his personality, and in some respects given strength that he does not have. Before the fall, headship and equality were so intricately interwoven that it was difficult to separate the two. But sin changed all that, affecting both men and women. Headship and submission needed to be emphasized and accentuated because of the problem of depravity.

But in Christ there is a certain restoration. A Christian man and wife have the potential to experience a unity and oneness that can grow constantly deeper and more meaningful day by day. Spiritually, there is total equality. But functionally, man is the head and the woman is to submit to his authority. Sin, of course, has not been eradicated, even through conversion. But in Christ, if a husband and wife continually and regularly fulfill their God-ordained roles, they have the potential to experience a foretaste of heaven on this side of glory. But this is a two-way street, and in the next chapter we'll see more clearly what it means for husbands to love as Christ loves.

The Twentieth-Century Dilemma

Why is it that many women today are seeking to be liberated? Why are so many unhappy with their roles, striving for equality in all aspects of life? The most significant reason goes back to a basic and root cause—sin. When sin entered the world, it not only affected all of us personally, but it affected the whole world in which we live.

First, on the non-Christian side of life, men have been notorious throughout history for using women for their own ends. On the current scene we see the playboy philosophy that views women as toys, as playthings, as means to selfish pleasure. No wonder most thinking women react against this self-centered philosophy. Today, more than ever before, women are used for materialistic business purposes. Sex sells anything, and women, of course, are the primary targets for this abuse. Again, it should not be surprising that thinking women would react to such selfish endeavors.

Women also react to the general male selfishness that permeates the whole society in which we live. Women have often been treated as inferior personalities, incapable of certain roles. They have often been "kept in their place" because men have been threatened by their abilities. Again, it should not surprise us that women can see through such egocentric behavior.

But where can these women turn? What is their source of authority for what they do? Unfortunately, most do not have, or they reject, the divine perspective. Motivated by the same sinful nature that motivates men, they are seeking liberation without God's principles. They do not realize that without Jesus Christ they can never know true freedom. Consequently, they overreact, moving first in one direction and then another. It is no wonder that the world is filled with frustrated people, many sincerely trying, but never able to come to a knowledge of God's ways and the secret to what they are looking for.

Second, some Christian women are also frustrated. Again, we must realize that every Christian woman and every Christian man is still a victim of the sin nature. We tend toward selfishness—not unselfishness. And unfortunately, some Christian men, motivated by the same selfish goals as non-Christian men, use the Scriptures to achieve their egocentric needs. This, of course, can be more devastating to a woman's self-image and self-worth than if a non-Christian behaved in this way. From an unbeliever she would expect it, but not from her Christian husband.

But of course, women are to blame, too. They, like all human beings, resist authority. We all do. It is difficult to submit to someone else. It is only by God's grace and help that we can become what God wants us to be.

Third, we need to note another important factor

that is making it difficult for women to adjust to their role in life. It involves our whole cultural milieu. Young girls in our society are taught to be professionally oriented throughout their academic experiences. The concept of homemaking takes a decided back seat to the excitement of a professional career. Psychologically, nearly every woman is geared in another direction from that which God intended. What this says to Christian men is that we must be sensitive to this problem in women. It is a real one and we cannot ignore it. To simply put a woman down or to "put her in her place" will only accentuate the problem.

Every woman must also recognize her tendency to act the way she has been subtly conditioned to act throughout her academic career. Together a husband and wife must face the reality of this problem, and within the context of Christian principles, work toward a satisfactory solution.

Life Response

1. As a husband or wife, take a moment to evaluate your attitudes. Are they conformed to scriptural principles? As a woman, do you understand your role? Are you overreacting in some way? And as a man, do you understand your wife? Do you understand her struggles? What are you doing to help her become a submissive wife?

2. As a single person, how are you being subtly influenced by this world's system? How do your present attitudes reflect a value system foreign to the Scriptures? Are you counterbalancing this negative influence with the true teachings of Scripture?

Remember that before you can find true happiness in marriage, you must be truly liberated in Jesus Christ.

Family or Group Project
Discuss this chapter with your family or small group. Remember: Now is the time to begin instilling principles of marriage in your children. If Christian parents do not counterbalance the world's value system, no one will.

4 THE CHRISTIAN HUSBAND
AND HEADSHIP

"Submission" emerges as a key word used in Scripture to describe a woman's relationship to a man. There can be no doubt that this is an important concept in the mind and plan of God—if indeed the Bible is inspired by God and accurate! And I believe it is!

True, submission has been woefully misinterpreted by Christians and non-Christians alike, in the home and in the church. On the one hand, some have used the word exclusively for women, which the Bible never does. The term is also used to describe a man's relationship to his wife. As Christians who make up Christ's body, we are *all* to submit to each other (see Eph. 5:21). And when the word "submission" *is* used to describe an exclusive role for women, it is often interpreted to mean "submission without qualifications." But the Bible does not support such thinking.

These misinterpretations of submission are wrong; but so is the attempt to eliminate altogether the concepts of submission and headship on the basis of culture and its negative and lingering influence on some biblical writers—especially the apostle Paul. This view poses many problems regarding the reliability of Scripture. True, understanding cultural factors is important in a proper exegetical treatment of Scripture. But to do away with headship in the marriage relationship is, it seems, an attempt by some to interpret the Bible in light of current movements in the world today—particularly the Women's Liberation Movement. And furthermore, it is a reaction against the extreme and unfortunate views of some Bible-believing Christians. Like so many, these interpreters have fallen sway to the "peril of the pendulum." They have swung too far, and, like the extremists they are reacting against, they too have made the Bible teach something it does not. In fact, I feel that it is not necessary to do away with the concept of biblical headship in order to have the practical benefits of an egalitarian relationship. Jesus Christ Himself gave an important clue in helping us understand this unique concept when He demonstrated His own humility by washing the disciples' feet. With this act of love, He was demonstrating that he that is greatest is also a servant (see John 13:12-17).

To understand the husband-wife relationship as it is described in Scripture, we must have a comprehensive view of the Word of God. We began in the previous chapter to show what the Bible teaches about submission. But we cannot clearly understand this biblical concept without a clear perspective regarding the concept of headship. Marriage is a two-way street, and you cannot define *wife*-husband relationships without looking carefully at *husband*-wife relationships.

Headship—What It Is Not

The Bible teaches that the husband is to occupy the position of headship in marriage. Paul clearly stated this when he reminded women to submit to their husbands as to the Lord. "For," said he, "the husband is the *head* of the wife as Christ is the *head* of the church" (Eph. 5:22,23).

What is "headship"? What does Paul mean? Again, it is usually helpful to look at what the Bible *doesn't* mean before attempting to state what it *does* mean.

Headship is not "dictatorship." There are some men—even Christian men—who use the concept of headship to justify authoritarian attitudes and behavior in marriage. They try to run their home like an egocentric army sergeant. They shout orders, demand instant obedience to every whim and wish, and meet opposition with psychological, if not physical, force. This is not "headship"—it's childishness and selfishness. It is the opposite of love.

Headship doesn't guarantee automatic respect. It is true that God has *given* man a position of headship in the home. But this does not guarantee that his wife (nor his children) will automatically respect and honor him from the heart. If a woman tries to recognize her husband's position of authority in her life, she will have difficulty following through at the feeling level if he does not, as Peter exhorts, treat her "with respect" (1 Pet. 3:7). Respect begets respect. Practically speaking, it is earned, even though God *gives* man the position. How man handles this sacred trust determines to a great extent whether or not he will indeed be the respected head of his household.

Headship doesn't mean the husband should make all the decisions. Nowhere in the Bible does God say the man should be the sole decision-maker in the home. Although the concept of headship certainly involves authority, it does not imply that a wife is incapable of making decisions, nor does it mean she should not be significantly involved in the process.

But more about the practical aspects of this idea later. Right now, the question before us is: *What does the Bible mean by "headship"?* As with most ideas in Scripture, a careful look at the text and context in which a concept appears reveals the true nature and meaning of that concept. And headship is no exception.

The key that unlocks the true meaning of biblical headship is Christ. Paul made this crystal clear when he said: "For the husband is the head of his wife *as Christ* is the head of the church" (Eph. 5:23). And again, "Husbands, love your wives, just *as Christ* loved the church" (Eph. 5:25).

Headship—a Divine Analogy

Paul, when writing to the Ephesian Christians about headship in the marital relationship, used a unique and dynamic analogy—an analogy of Jesus Christ and His relationship to the Church. Just as Christ is the head of the Church, so the husband is to be the head of the wife. Just as Christ loved the Church, so the husband is to love his wife!

The analogy—it's limitations. When an analogy is used as a communication technique (as Paul does in Eph. 5), its basic purpose is to explain more clearly the meaning of some idea or concept. And the concept Paul was explaining to the Ephesian Christians focused on the true meaning of headship in marriage. His analogy was that of Christ and the Church.

The average dictionary defines "analogy" as "similarity in some respects" or "partial resemblance." In other words, no analogy, no matter how effective, can convey the totality of the idea being explained. If you try to make it "walk on all fours," you'll come up with an incorrect interpretation, or in some instances, an impossible situation.

This is true of Paul's analogy in Ephesians 5. Its limitations are immediately obvious when the true meaning of Christ's headship and love for the Church are clearly understood.

First, Christ had (and always has had) *absolute authority.* As Paul explained to the Colossians, Christ "is the image of the invisible God, the firstborn over all creation. For by him all things were created: things in heaven and on earth, visible and invisible, whether thrones or powers or rulers or authorities; all things were created by him and for him. He is before all things, and in him all things hold together" (Col. 1:15-17).

And, in the very context of describing Christ's absolute authority over all creation, Paul goes on to mention His headship—that "he is the *head of the body*, the church; he is the beginning and the firstborn from among the dead, so that in everything he might have supremacy" (v. 18).

Paul's analogy, of course, cannot convey to a Christian husband that he, like Christ, has *absolute* authority. True, he does have authority, but that authority must be carefully interpreted and defined in the light of the limitations God places on man in other parts of the Word of God.

Second, Christ was *perfect* in His attitudes and actions. He never sinned. Though He was truly man, His love for us was never marred by human weakness. Though He was tempted to be selfish, He never was. Though He was tempted to envy, to be rude, to be proud, to be easily angered, He never allowed these feelings to manifest themselves in persistent attitudes and behavior that was characterized by unrighteousness. Though He was "tempted in every way, just as we are," still He was "without sin" (Heb. 4:15). He was indeed God in human form.

Paul's analogy, then—like all analogies—has certain limitations. No man has absolute authority nor is he without sin. What, then, is Paul saying?

The analogy—it's true meaning. Though no man can function in all respects as Christ functioned, yet God has made it possible for every Christian to become more and more conformed to Christ's image (see 2 Cor. 3:18). This is God's plan. He is our divine example. And His Spirit, working through the Word of God and other members of the body of Christ, is our divine source of power, encouragement, and enablement. It is indeed possible to imitate Christ, though we will never be like Him in all respects, even in eternity.

Paul, of course, believed this. If he didn't, he would never have instructed the Corinthians to imitate his life as he, Paul, imitated Christ's life (see 1 Cor. 11:1). And he would not have ordered the Ephesians to "be imitators of God" and to "live a life of love, just as Christ loved us and gave himself for us" (Eph. 5:1,2). And more specifically—and directly relevant to the subject at hand—he would not have exhorted Christian husbands living in Ephesus to love their wives "just as Christ loved the church and gave himself up for her" (Eph. 5:25).

It is possible, then, for Christian husbands to love as Christ loved—not in the fullest and most comprehensive meaning of that concept—but as much as is humanly possible with divine enablement that comes through Christian conversion and spiritual growth. And though we will always fail in some measure and sin against our wives, we can, and should, experience overall progress in this God-ordained process.

Some Specific Christlike Attitudes and Actions

How can a Christian husband love his wife as Christ loved the Church? What must he be—and do? To be in the will of God, what must characterize his attitudes and behavior?

Paul succinctly summarized the answers to these questions when writing to the Philippian Christians. And again we see the parallel between the home and the Church, for here—in Philippians 2—he was talking generally to every member of Christ's body.

First, Paul gave a specific exhortation. "Do nothing," he said, "out of selfish ambition or vain conceit, but in humility consider others better than yourselves. Each of you should look not only to your own interests, but also to the interests of others" (Phil. 2:3,4).

Then, to get his point across clearly, Paul used the very same analogy he used in Ephesians 5—Christ and the Church. "Your attitude," he said, "should be the same as that of Christ Jesus" (v. 5). But then as Paul developed this analogy, he got even more specific than he did in Ephesians 5. He actually spelled out what that attitude should be.

An attitude of unselfishness. "Your attitude should be the same as that of Christ Jesus: Who, being in very nature God, did not consider equality with God something to be grasped" (Phil. 2:5,6). In other words, Christ did not cling to His heavenly position with the Father, but was willing to lay it aside to come into this world—the world He made. And in His incarnation, He identified with our fallen condition, though He, of course, did not personally participate in sin. He did, however, give up the glories of heaven to live among men. And when He did so, He was demonstrating an unselfish attitude that is unparalleled in the universe.

An attitude of humility. (See Phil. 2:7.) Christ, who was "in very nature God," voluntarily "made himself nothing." He, who created all things, temporarily laid aside His heavenly glory. He, who was and is God, took upon Himself "the very nature of a servant." He, who made man, took upon Himself "human likeness." This, of course, is ultimate humility personified.

An attitude of sacrifice and self-giving. Jesus Christ demonstrated the greatest act of love ever known to mankind. "Being found in appearance as a man, he humbled himself and became obedient to death—even death on a cross!" (Phil. 2:8). Jesus Christ died that we might live. Because man's sin demanded the penalty of death, Jesus Christ died for every man—even His enemies. Thus when they nailed Him to the cross, He prayed—"Father, forgive them, for they do not know what they are doing" (Luke 23:34).

From Analogy to Action

Paul's analogy, in his Philippian letter, is a powerful demonstration and elaboration of what he meant when he exhorted husbands to "love as Christ loved."

An attitude of unselfishness. Like Jesus, a Christian husband should not grasp and hold on to his position of authority, using it as a manipulative device to get what he wants. True, there may be times when he must make decisions and judgments that will cause a certain amount of resistance and even emotional pain, but he must always use his authority for the benefit of his mate—and his children. As Paul wrote to the Colossians, he must "not be harsh" with his wife (Col. 3:19). Nor should he discourage his children (see Col. 3:21). And whatever he does must be done to protect his wife, to assist her in her personal growth. Christ's goal for the Church is to "make her holy . . . to present her to himself as a radiant church, without stain or wrinkle or any other blemish, but holy and blameless. In this same way," continued Paul, "husbands ought to love their wives as their own bodies. He who loves his wife loves himself" (Eph. 5:26-28).

An attitude of humility. Though God has given

65

man a position of headship and authority, he must realize that he is also a servant. He must never lord it over his wife, using his male ego as an excuse for insensitivity and personal defensiveness that is purely self-protection.

Furthermore, he must identify with his wife—her pain, her heartaches, her struggles, her weaknesses, her anxieties, her stresses. Remember that Christ's love caused Him to identify with us. To love your wife as Christ loved the Church means identification with her. In fact, Peter laid on Christian husbands the heaviest injunction of all—"Husbands, in the same way be considerate as you live with your wives, and treat them with respect as the weaker partner and as heirs with you of the gracious gift of life, so that nothing will hinder your prayers" (1 Pet. 3:7). There is no question what Peter had in mind. We must identify with their weaknesses and we must understand and minister to them. Furthermore, Peter actually stipulates that some men's prayers are hindered because they do not "love their wives as Christ loved the church."

How unfortunate when people conclude that God is against women, that He is unfair, and that Paul's teaching particularly opens the door for male insensitivity and unchecked authority. True, because of sin some Christian men are very insensitive. "But," says the Lord, "I won't answer their prayers." This represents God's most significant check on male authority.

An attitude of sacrifice and self-giving. This is one of the most difficult facets of Paul's analogy. When it comes to sacrifice, most of us operate at a very superficial level. Much of what we do—if we're not careful—is for ourselves. It may appear on the surface to be for the benefit of our mate, but a closer look into the depths of our psychological nature reveals a person we'd rather not see.

But interestingly, Paul seems to recognize this as a human weakness in men (and all Christians)—one that is difficult to overcome, except by redirecting our selfish orientation. Thus he said: "Husbands ought to love their wives as their own bodies. He who loves his wife loves himself. After all, no one ever hated his own body, but he feeds and cares for it, just as Christ does the church—for we are members of his body" (Eph. 5:28-30).

Life Response

Paul, in writing to the Philippians, was directing his exhortations to all Christians in order that they might demonstrate three basic attitudes: (1) unselfishness, (2) humility, and (3) sacrifice, self-giving. In light of these qualities evaluate your own life. Where are you in the process of being able to "love as Christ loved"? Check the items that most adequately describe your life-style.

Note: If you are a Christian husband, you can zero in on your relationship to your wife.

   I. Unselfishness:
      ☐ Basically unselfish
      ☐ More unselfish than selfish
      ☐ More selfish than unselfish
      ☐ Basically selfish
   II. Humility:
      ☐ Basically humble and meek
      ☐ More humble than arrogant

□ More arrogant than humble
□ Basically arrogant and proud

III. Sacrificial:
□ Basically sacrificial
□ More sacrificial than self-centered and egotistical
□ More self-centered and egotistical than sacrificial
□ Basically self-centered and egotistical

Family or Group Project

Have each member of your family (or group) run the preceding test on themselves after reviewing the material in this chapter. Then pray together, asking God to help you become a truly loving person and to eliminate from your personality the qualities that are not Christlike.

Note: For a very personal husband-wife project, evaluate how you *feel* about your mate and share your responses with each other.

Warning: Be prepared to face some threatening realities. However, it could be a basic step that will change your life.

5 CHRISTIAN CHILDREN
AND OBEDIENCE

In the midst of a world where the majority of people are bent on doing their own thing, obedience is not a popular topic. But that shouldn't be surprising. Obedience has always been difficult. Ever since God created man, obedience has been a problem. Even before sin entered the world, man had the potential to disobey—and he did! It was Eve who first disobeyed God, and Adam followed close behind. Their act of disobedience plunged the whole world into sin—an act that has seriously affected every human being since that day. If Adam and Eve chose to disobey God *before* the Fall, it shouldn't be too surprising that disobedience became an accentuated problem *after* the Fall.

As we've already seen from previous chapters, the

entrance of sin into the world seriously affected family relationships. Generally speaking, submission and love were unknown concepts in pagan marriages. Selfishness, arrogance, and egocentric behavior reigned in the hearts of both men and women. Thus Paul, in writing to the Ephesian Christians, included Christian wives and husbands when he exhorted them to "no longer live as the Gentiles do" (Eph. 4:17). Becoming very specific, he wrote to wives: "Submit to your husbands as to the Lord" (Eph. 5: 22). And to husbands, he said: "Love your wives, just as Christ loved the church" (Eph. 5:25).

But the entrance of sin into the world also affected other relationships that eventually evolve in nearly every marriage—the relationship between children and parents. And in Paul's letter to the Roman Christians, he spoke directly to this point. First, Paul wrote generally about the deteriorating effects of sin in the lives of all men: "They have become filled with every kind of wickedness, evil, greed and depravity. They are full of envy, murder, strife, deceit and malice. They are gossips, slanderers, God-haters, insolent, arrogant and boastful; they invent ways of doing evil" (Rom. 1:29,30).

And then, Paul specifically describes the effects of sin on child/parent relationships. Speaking of children, Paul wrote, "They *disobey their parents;* they are senseless, faithless, heartless, ruthless" (Rom. 1:30,31).

Many pagan families who were converted to Christ in the New Testament world were formerly characterized by the very traits enumerated by Paul in this paragraph in his Roman letter. And the Ephesian and

70

Colossian Christians were no exception (see Eph. 4:17-24; Col. 3:5-11). Thus Paul not only instructed husbands and wives regarding the new relationship that should exist between them, but he also exhorted children regarding the new attitudes and actions they should have toward their parents: "Children, obey your parents in the Lord, for this is right. 'Honor your father and mother'—which is the first commandment with a promise—'that it may go well with you and that you may enjoy a long life on the earth' " (Eph. 6:1-3). To the Colossians Paul said: "Children, obey your parents in everything, for this pleases the Lord" (Col. 3:20).

Paul gives four reasons why children should obey their parents. However, before we look at these four reasons, note that the word translated "children" in this passage does not refer to *small* children. Rather, Paul was speaking of children who were no doubt teenagers or older—children who were old enough and mature enough to be responsible for their actions. One of the most obvious reasons for this conclusion is that Paul in this letter actually directed his comments to children personally, assuming that they would be old enough to understand a rather profound injunction.

Secondly, the Greek word for children, *teknon*, is used quite frequently in the New Testament to refer to offspring in general. And the context in which the word appears usually makes it very clear that older children are involved. In fact, in some instances it's obvious that Paul is talking about grown, adult children.

This is an important observation. Many Christians,

71

misusing some of these verses that refer to teenagers and older children, try to train and discipline small children in ways they are not yet ready to handle. This often leads to serious behavioral problems, making obedience even more difficult for the child when he grows older. (More on this topic in chapter 8.)

Let's look now at the reasons Paul gives for children to obey and honor their parents.

Doctrinal Reasons

The first two reasons Paul gives for obedience in the Ephesian letter are based on doctrinal truths.

Because you're Christians. (See Eph. 6:1.) This, I believe, is what Paul meant when he said: "Obey your parents *in the Lord.*" Some have translated: "Obey your parents *because of the Lord.*" And in his Colossian letter, Paul perhaps made it even clearer: "Children, obey your parents in everything, for *this pleases the Lord.*"

Some people have interpreted Paul's statement in the Ephesian letter to mean that children should obey only when their parents are Christians—in other words, when their parents are "in the Lord." This, it seems, is not an accurate interpretation. Paul certainly would not exempt Christian children from obedience just because their parents were yet pagans, any more than he would exempt wives from submission just because their husbands were not yet saved. In fact, as Peter did in his epistle when writing to wives (see 1 Pet. 3:1-6), Paul would probably have accentuated the importance of obedience under those circumstances.

No, this does not seem to be the true meaning. Paul

is simply repeating in a concise way something he had already clearly elaborated on earlier in his letter when speaking to all believers. Because you're now Christians, he is saying, because you have a new position in Christ, because you are no longer darkened in your understanding and "separated from the life of God" (Eph. 4:18), therefore, "put off your old self, which is being corrupted by its deceitful desires; to be made new in the attitude of your minds." You should "put on the new self, created to be like God in true righteousness and holiness" (Eph. 4:22-24). And of course, Paul becomes very specific when he said: "Get rid of all bitterness, rage and anger, brawling and slander, along with every form of malice. Be kind and compassionate to one another, forgiving each other, just as in Christ God forgave you" (Eph. 4:31, 32).

To summarize, the first reason Paul gives children for obeying their parents is because of their *position in Christ.* They were "in the Lord." Their lives were no longer their own. They were bought with the precious blood of Christ, and along with their parents, they were now a part of a *new* family—"the family of God."

Because it's the right thing to do. "Children, obey your parents in the Lord," wrote Paul, *"for this is right"* (Eph. 6:1). As a young man just ready to enter His teen years, Jesus Christ set an outstanding example of obedience to His parents (see Luke 2:41-51). Each year, as a family, they traveled to Jerusalem to take part in the Passover Feast. When the event was over, His parents were on their way back with their friends and relatives, and had been on their way for

73

one whole day before they noticed that Jesus was not in the crowd. They returned to Jerusalem immediately, but it was three days before they found Jesus. He was in the Temple talking with the teachers of the Law. In fact, His questions and answers were so profound that He astonished these men, who were, themselves, experts in understanding and interpreting the law of Moses.

By this time, of course, Jesus' parents (particularly His mother) were nearly beside themselves. And after some rather emotional comments by Mary, Jesus responded with complete obedience.

Here again, we see Jesus Christ setting the great example in how to live as a Christian. In our last chapter we mentioned His unselfish, humble, and self-giving attitudes and actions in leaving heaven's glory to become a man in order to be the Saviour of the world. And here in this story we see Him, at age 12, even with all of His wisdom and knowledge, setting an outstanding example for all youth to observe and imitate—obedience to parents. Though He already knew why He came into the world, and that He was the Son of God, He submitted Himself to His parents' authority.

Obedience to parents, then, is the *right thing to do*. Paul's reasoning was based on the example of Jesus Christ Himself.

Personal Reasons

There are also some very personal and practical reasons for children to obey their parents. And to make his point, Paul referred to one of the Ten Commandments given to Israel by God years before when they were at Mount Sinai in the wilderness. " 'Honor your father and mother'—which," explained Paul, "is the first commandment with a promise" (Eph. 6:2). In other words, Paul pointed out to the young people at Ephesus that obedience to parents is so important in God's sight that He actually included a promise with this command—some "personal benefits" if you will.

This promise, of course, was first given to the children of Israel and involved special blessings in the land of Canaan. But Paul, speaking with the authority of the Holy Spirit, generalized this promise to include personal benefits for *all* Christians who obey their parents.

What, then, are these benefits?

" *'That it may go well with you.'* " (Eph. 6:3). It would not be accurate or fair to tell all young people that if they obey their parents life for them will always be a rose garden. Paul certainly was not giving some magic formula for total happiness. But experience certainly verifies the fact that *most* children who obey and honor their parents do themselves a tremendous favor. Cruel indeed—and rare—are parents who respond to obedient children with greater restrictions and harshness. Rather, the opposite is usually true. The way to greater freedom and trust is obedience and respect.

In other words, do you want your parents to trust you? Then honor and obey them. Do you want things to go well with you? Then demonstrate to your parents that you love them, that you appreciate them, that you want to please them, and that you want to make life easy for them. Nothing is more frustrating to a parent than to have to hassle with his own flesh and blood. And of course, nothing is more frustrating for a young person than to be in a power struggle with his parents. Paul says that obedience and honor are the keys to overcoming much of this difficulty. Do yourself a favor then, and obey your parents! You'll do them a favor, too!

There *are* exceptions to this rule. Just as there are children who are so self-centered that they will not respond positively to parental love, so there are parents who are so "out of it" spiritually and emotionally, that they will only take advantage of children who obey and honor them. And in these cases, the Bible does not teach unqualified obedience, any more than it teaches that a wife must forever submit herself to a cruel, domineering and sick husband.

The Bible teaches by precept and example that "we must obey God rather than men" (Acts 5:29). This was the apostles' response to the religious leaders in Jerusalem who commanded them to stop preaching the gospel. In other words, if a parent demands that one of his children violate a commandment of God, he must choose to obey God first. God is a higher authority than parents.

But let me warn you! Make sure that the demand is indeed a violation of God's Word. It's easy to rationalize our behavior when we really want to go our own way. Futhermore, before you actually disobey your parents, consult your pastor or other mature Christians in your church if at all possible. Seek their advice as to what to do. Mature Christian adults who are not subjectively involved can often give you unusual wisdom in seeking a solution to this kind of problem. Consider the following example:

A young man wanted to be baptized, but his non-Christian parents would not give their permission. He came to me for advice. With his permission, I called his home to talk with his parents about it. Only his mother was home, but I explained to her that we did not want to encourage her son to disobey them since they *were* his parents. I explained the true meaning of baptism and also offered to be willing to help in any way to clarify communication between them and their son.

A couple of days later, I received a call from the boy's father, who had returned home from a business trip. His wife evidently had told him about my call, and that I had sought permission to baptize the boy—but that I would not do it without their permission. Because of this approach, the father had a complete change of heart and called to give permission for his boy to be baptized.

The point is—when in difficulty, consult mature members of the body of Christ to get advice and help. It is a pastor's responsibility to help Christian young people who are in difficulty with their parents. If your parents are actually sinning against you in unjust ways, even though you are attempting to be obedient, it is the responsibility of the leaders in your church, in love, to help you solve the problem.

"That you may enjoy long life on the earth" (Eph. 6:3). Does Paul actually mean a young person is guaranteed a "long life" if he obeys his parents? Not necessarily. Again, this is no magic formula.

There are some people who live a long, long time on this earth, even though they disobey their parents.

But because they ignored their parents' advice, they spend the rest of their days as miserable, unhappy people. Think of the young people who did not consult their parents' advice about marriage, and ignored the advice they got when they did consult them—and then proceeded to marry a person who was immature and irresponsible, and in some instances, not even a Christian. And today they are divorced, brokenhearted, and bitter. And if the home has not broken up, they are trying hard to make the best of a miserable marriage in order not to violate the will of God a second time.

Some have had opportunity to start over, but some will never totally overcome the heartache. Some make a worse decision the second time around. Unfortunately, one major act of disobedience sometimes starts people in the direction of a whole series of bad decisions and mistakes.

This is just one illustration of how disobedience can lead to heartache rather than happiness; how ignoring advice and counsel can lead to a long life on earth that is filled with sorrow and pain. In fact, some people are so miserable they wish they were dead.

But there's also a literal aspect to this promise to "enjoy long life on the earth." Though the Lord is not *guaranteeing* a long life, He is making it quite clear that disobedient children can shorten their life on earth through foolish and irresponsible actions. In the first-century culture, running with the wrong crowd could easily lead to death, and the same is true in the twentieth-century world. Every day, young people die in car accidents, from overdoses of drugs, and from other causes because they have disobeyed their parents. And some, though they do not agree with what their friends do, become innocently involved because of their association with the wrong crowd. There are young people in prison today who did not pull the trigger, and who would never have pulled the trigger, but because they were there when it happened, they were classified as an accomplice.

There are, then, some very practical reasons for obedience to parents. It has always been true—in the days of Moses, in the days of Paul, and now in the latter days. As the world heads toward that great day when Jesus comes again, Christian children should set the example in obedience to parents.

"Mark this," wrote Paul to Timothy, "There will be terrible times in the last days. People will be lovers of themselves, lovers of money, boastful, proud, abusive, *disobedient to their parents . . . . Have nothing to do with them*" (2 Tim. 3:1-5).

Obedience—a Christian's Responsibility

Paul's exhortation in Ephesians 6:1-3 is directed specifically at children. But obedience is not a word used exclusively in the New Testament when referring to children, any more than the word submission is used exclusively for women or the word love is used exclusively for men. Obedience—like submission and love—are words used to describe Christian attitudes and actions for *all* members of Christ's body.

Obedience to employers. In the very same passage in which Paul exhorts children to obey their parents, he instructs slaves to obey their "earthly masters with respect and fear, and with sincerity of heart, just as

79

you would obey Christ" (Eph. 6:5). Applied to our culture, this means respecting and obeying our employers. As a parent, don't demand obedience from your children and then turn around and flaunt and disobey your employer. This is a contradiction and a violation of God's will. If your employer is unfair, in our culture we usually have channels to express our grievances, but we must do so with Christian grace. If your employer is intolerable, it's better to seek another position rather than to violate God's will. This, of course, is one of the blessings of living in America today. Slaves in the first century did not have this choice. They had no grievance committee.

Obedience to governing authorities. Christians have a responsibility to obey governing authorities. Paul makes this clear both in Romans 13:1 and in his letter to Titus: "Remind the people to be subject to rulers and authorities, *to be obedient*" (Titus 3:1).

In our time this means being honest in paying our income tax, obeying speed laws, stopping at stop signs and honoring other government regulations—even when they may not be to our liking. There is no place for violence and rebellion in God's plan for Christians. Proper channels for change, yes—another blessing of living in twentieth-century America—but never trying to take the law into our own hands. The only exception arises when Christians are commanded to do something that disobeys God. Then we must make a choice, but not with a rebellious or non-Christian attitude. Again, fortunately, in America today, Christians are very seldom asked to make that kind of choice. This is not true, however, in other sections of the world.

Obedience to church leaders. No doubt speaking of the elders of the church, the author of Hebrews wrote: "Obey your leaders and submit to their authority. They keep watch over you as men who must give an account. Obey them so that their work will be a joy, not a burden, for that would be of no advantage to you" (Heb. 13:17).

Elders who lead a local body of Christ are held responsible in God's plan for leading well just as parents are responsible for their children. As children are to obey parents, so members of the body of Christ are to obey and respect their elders.

Again, this does not mean obedience without qualification. Just as Paul directs some very strong statements at parents in their attitudes toward their children, he also instructs elders to be examples to the flock and not to lord it over those entrusted to them (see 1 Pet. 5:3). And once again, we see an unusual relationship within Christ's body. There can be mutual love, submission, honor, respect and obedience to each other—even within the context of recognized authority.

Life Response

In what area of your life are you experiencing difficulty with obedience?

☐ Obeying and honoring my parents

(Note: Once we've established our own family or are on our own as a single person, this does not exempt us from *honoring* our parents—though they certainly do not have the right to run our lives. But we must always love and honor them.)

☐ Obeying and honoring my employer

☐ Obeying and respecting government leaders and regulations

☐ Obeying and respecting my spiritual leaders

Write out one thing you're going to do immediately to correct an area of weakness in your Christian life.

Family or Group Project

Spend time reviewing this chapter. As parents, encourage your children—those who are old enough—to share their feelings about the rules and regulations in your household. Ask them if they feel they're fair. Listen carefully to what they say before sharing the reasons for the rules.

6 CHRISTIAN PARENTS
AND NURTURE

When my two daughters, who are now grown, were about four and five years old, I overheard them one day talking about God. On the surface their childlike comments seemed very simple, yet what they were talking about was indeed profound. Said one, with a sudden flash of insight and excitement, "You know, God is our heavenly Daddy."

Neither realized the implications of that statement. But their father, who was intently listening in the other room, certainly did. Suddenly I realized as never before that their view of God was their view of me. I, a *visible* father, was representing—rightly or wrongly—the *invisible* Father. Their experiential knowledge of God was not so much what I was *telling* them God was like, but rather what they were learning from my personality—my attitudes and behavior toward their mother, toward them, and toward other people.

Thus Paul, in his Ephesian and Colossian letters, directs his comments regarding child nurture particularly to fathers. "Fathers, do not exasperate your children; instead, bring them up in the training and instruction of the Lord" (Eph. 6:4; see also Col. 3:21).

Though Paul apparently was directing his exhortations primarily at fathers, a closer look at the original text and the New Testament culture seems to indicate that he is really speaking to both dad and mom. But in another sense, what he says *does* apply in a special way to fathers, because both the Old and New Testaments place a heavy responsibility for child nurture on fathers.

A father, in a very special way, represents the "God image" in the family structure. God is called our "heavenly Father"—not our "heavenly Mother" —though He certainly represents both parents in a unique way. Both man and woman are created in God's image (see Gen. 1:27). But from the beginning, man's authority and position in the family was identified more specifically with God's authority and position in the universe. Though its reality has certainly been perverted and changed in certain cultures where the "mother image" is more predominant, it was not so from the beginning. God's image in Scripture has always been more masculine then feminine. And, of course, the greatest manifestation of all was the coming to this earth of the *man* Christ Jesus, who was God in the flesh.

Thus Paul, in Ephesians 4, directed his exhortation

primarily to fathers, who are in a special way to represent Jesus Christ to their children.

When writing to New Testament fathers (and parents) in his Ephesian letter, Paul spoke first regarding what a father should *not* do; then he told them what *to* do. And together, these two brief and concise statements (both negative and positive) form a very comprehensive philosophy of parenting.

Fathers, Do Not Exasperate Your Children

In his Colossian letter, Paul elaborated a little more on what he meant by this statement. "Do not embitter your children," he warned, "or they will become discouraged" (Col. 3:21).

In the New Testament world, most pagan fathers were anything but sensitive to their children. In fact, Paul had already reminded them that in their former way of life they had "lost all sensitivity" (Eph. 4:19). They were abusive in their speech, often reflecting "bitterness, rage, and anger" (Eph. 4:29,30; see also Col. 3:8). Knowing our own tendency toward impatience and also being aware of what is happening in the present culture regarding child abuse (a number one problem in America), it doesn't take too much imagination to reconstruct what was happening in some of the family structures in the New Testament world. Therefore, Paul is once again reminding the Ephesians—this time parents—that they are now Christians. They should no longer live as the Gentiles do.

But what about modern Christian fathers and mothers? In what ways can we exasperate, embitter, and discourage our children?

85

When we abuse them physically. There is no place for brutal discipline in a Christian family—or any family. Discipline, yes. And to set the record straight, spanking too! But always in love and for the benefit of the child. I've known Christian parents who have struck their children with their fists, and whipped small children so severely that they hurt for days. Common sense tells us this is wrong and sinful. Paul's warnings directly apply to these situations.

This often happens to parents because they are venting their hostility on their children. It is one thing to be angry with a child, but still another to be so deeply angry at others and at ourselves that we are transferring our hostility to our children. When this happens, we are not disciplining in love. In fact, we have some serious psychological and spiritual problems.

When we abuse them psychologically. Some parents would never think of physically striking their children in brutal ways, but they use words to achieve similar results. Children can be destroyed psychologically by an adult who humiliates them and puts them down. In many cases, this kind of abuse leads to more anger, bitterness, and discouragement in children than physical abuse. It is far more lethal and long-range in its negative effects.

When we neglect them. This is particularly relevant to the contemporary American father. We can get so busy in our business, social, and even church life that we have little or no time left for our children. Neglect also creates resentment and bitterness.

People in the ministry often have double trouble. We can get so busy ministering to other people—and other people's children—that we have no time to be with our own children. The children of many pastors and missionaries have become hostile and resentful toward their parents because they have been neglected. And in some instances, they transfer that bitterness to the Bible and to the Lord.

This should not be too difficult to understand. It was because of the parents' "serving the Lord" and "teaching the Word of God" that the child felt neglected. The natural tendency is to resent what took his parent away from him. In this case, psychological problems become severe spiritual problems.

When we don't understand them. It's easy to make judgments and decisions without understanding the child's point of view. And when children are misunderstood, they resent it, just as we resent it when people misunderstand us.

It takes effort to understand children—especially in our changing culture. Many of them have problems that are different from ours when we were their age. Their basic needs are the same, but the way these needs are met often is culturally conditioned.

Listen to your children. Don't become so preoccupied with your own world and your own needs that you don't even know what they're doing, what they're concerned about, and what their real problems are. If you don't know them and understand them, you'll not make proper decisions that affect them positively.

When we expect too much from them. Some parents set standards so high for their children that they are constantly frustrated. This also eventually leads to anger and discouragement.

Be realistic. Children's performance and ability levels vary with age level and with different personalities. Don't even expect the same from every child in your family.

And by all means, don't try to achieve through your children, meeting your own ego needs that went unmet when you were a child. This is devastating to a child's self-concept and image. And he'll resent you for it.

When we put them on a performance standard. This is a great source of frustration in many children. If they conform to the parent's standard, they are loved and accepted. If they do not, they are punished and rejected. This, too, results in hostility. And what is even more tragic, the child learns to interpret God in the same way. Thus he reasons, "If I'm good, He'll accept me and favor me. If I'm bad, He'll reject me and punish me."

This, of course, is not a true reflection of God's unconditional love. It is a reflection of an inconsistent parent. God does discipline us, yes, but always for our own good. But never does He reject us, for we are always accepted in His sight if we know Jesus Christ as our personal Saviour.

When we force them to accept our goals and ideas. This is a difficult problem. As parents, we feel we know best—and, in many cases, we do. But children —particularly in their teen and young adult years— must eventually make their own decisions about vocational goals, social relationships, and even their faith. These things we cannot force without negative reactions.

Don't misunderstand! If, as they are growing up,

we have been the example we should have been, if we have taught them the truth they should know, if we have truly lived Jesus Christ before them, they will never get away from that impact. Even when they are in a period of doubt, ordinarily they will eventually accept our views, our life-style, and our faith—particularly if it is properly reflecting the Word of God. But it must be an *inward* decision on their part. Don't force it. Teach it, yes! But sensitively, and with a listening ear. Be glad when they share with you their doubts and fears and problems. It's a tribute to the security they feel with you. Don't destroy it by being defensive and emotional.

When we won't admit our own mistakes. One of the hardest things for a parent to do is to admit his own mistakes—to say "I'm sorry." When a parent blows it, the child usually knows it. Don't hesitate to apologize or to ask for forgiveness. You won't lose respect. Rather, you'll win it. And you'll be teaching by example a great biblical truth. If we don't admit our mistakes, most children sense it and their respect for us can be destroyed.

"Bring Them Up in the Lord"

Paul turned next from those things parents *should not do* to those things they *should do.* And there are two basic ways to nurture children—by example and by direct instruction and teaching. Paul, no doubt, had both in mind in this verse.

By example. The most powerful way to teach young children is by parental example. If our relationships with our children are good, if they feel comfortable with us, if they love us, they naturally want to be like us, particularly as they enter the third year of life. They will talk like us, and even their tone of voice will sound like ours. If we're loud and boisterous and yell a lot, they become the same way. If we are sensitive, honest, and understanding, they learn to reflect the same qualities. Putting it simply, if we want our children to reflect Jesus Christ in their lifestyle, we must be good examples of Jesus Christ.

By direct instruction. Paul used a beautiful illustration of parental instruction in 1 Thessalonians. He was talking about his own ministry with these Thessalonian Christians, but he used an analogy from the home. Note what he said: "For you know that we dealt with each of you as a *father deals with his own children*, encouraging, comforting and urging you to live lives worthy of God, who calls you into his kingdom and glory" (1 Thess. 2:11,12).

This is a powerful illustration. First, Paul demonstrated what he believed the father should do with *each one* of his children. In other words, he was saying we must touch each child's life personally, meeting his own individual needs. We must never just rear a family, but each child in that family.

But notice also the process! "We dealt with each of you," wrote Paul, "*encouraging, comforting* and *urging* you to live lives worthy of God."

Parents should constantly *encourage* their children —not discourage them. We must give them positive feedback, we must let them know we're interested in their interests; we must let them know that we're proud of their accomplishments, that we love them unconditionally, no matter what their problems.

Many children are never noticed unless they do

something bad. No wonder some children create problems to get attention. Some are even willing to suffer the results of severe discipline in order to get attention. How unfortunate when this becomes a pattern in a child's life! And how tragic—and frustrating —when parents don't recognize what has happened.

One of the most important ministries a parent can have with children is to *comfort* them when they are hurting—both physically and emotionally. We must be able to identify with their hurts and even their anger.

How frequently a child comes home from school, angry, hurt and bitter toward a teacher or other children. Often the first thing he hears from his parents is that he shouldn't *feel* that way. But also how frequently that anger can be dissipated and dealt with by a parent who identifies with his hurt, who says, for example: "You must have had a very difficult day today. Tell me about it."

When a child has had a difficult day, his feelings are the same as an adult who has also had a difficult day. Like an adult, when he is misunderstood or embarrassed, he becomes hurt and angry.

A parent's responsibility is to comfort children, to help them express their feelings, even though these may be hostile feelings, and then to help them develop a proper perspective on the problem.

Most children's feelings are based on quite understandable reasons. The child lives in a cruel world, and often he gets caught in the midst of adult inconsistencies and weaknesses. Then *he* often gets blamed for it. No wonder his feelings are not always positive.

Paul's final reflection on his own ministry from a

father's point of view emphasizes motivation. Here Paul is talking about *encouraging children to live lives that are worthy of God*—that are "holy, righteous, and blameless." And notice that Paul's analogy grows out of the previous verse, where he and his fellow missionaries demonstrated with their lives these three basic Christian qualities (see 1 Thess. 2:10).

Again, the motivation to live a righteous and godly life comes from both example and direct teaching. We must never hesitate to warn our children of sin, of its dangers, and of its devastating effects. This is part of our teaching responsibility. We must teach them God's Word. They must understand that the only true way to find happiness is to find our rest in God, by doing His will, and by living lives that please Him.

A Word to All Christians

Interestingly, we again see that Christian nurture and concern is not an exclusive responsibility for parents. In a sense, all believers are to "parent" each other. We are *not* to "slander one another" (Jas. 4:11), nor to "grumble against one another" (Jas. 5:9). Neither are we to pass "judgment on one another" (Rom. 14:13). Rather, we are *all* to "teach and counsel one another" (Col. 3:16). We are to "encourage one another daily" (Heb. 3:13). And we are all to "consider how we may spur one another on toward love and good deeds" (Heb. 10:24).

In these exhortations to all Christians we see the same basic responsibilities that parents have for children. These attitudes lead to harmony and unity, not anger, bitterness, and discouragement.

Life Response

1. As a parent, where are you strong and where do you need to improve? Put a plus (+) by those areas where you feel good about your attitudes and behavior. Put a minus (−) where you feel a need for improvement.

☐ Proper discipline void of physical abuse

☐ Proper discipline void of psychological abuse

☐ Not neglecting them in terms of time

☐ Understanding their needs and problems

☐ Not expecting too much from them

☐ Avoiding putting them on a performance standard

☐ Not *forcing* goals and desires on them, but setting a proper example with good teaching and a Christlike life-style

☐ Admitting mistakes and asking for forgiveness

☐ Showing personal interest and concern for each child

☐ Giving adequate encouragement

☐ Giving adequate comfort

☐ Giving adequate motivation to live godly lives

2. As a member of Christ's body, what can you do to teach, encourage, comfort, and motivate another member of Christ's body? Be specific. Write out a goal for this week. Select someone you know who is in need.

Family or Group Project

As a husband and wife, discuss your areas of strength and weakness. Share your responses to the above checklist with each other. Together, set new goals for ministering to your children. Be sure to be specific.

As a member of Christ's body generally, call a friend or several friends and together decide what you can do to help a discouraged member of Christ's body.

7 FAMILY NURTURE
AN OLD TESTAMENT MODEL

Paul made it clear that Christian parents are primarily responsible to nurture their children. And he also illustrated with his own life, as he ministered to believers in general, what he believed this process should be (see 1 Thess. 2:11,12). Interestingly—but not surprisingly—the Old Testament gives us a more detailed model of *how* to bring children up in the instruction and training of the Lord. And a unique model it is! It includes all the major problems, frustrations, and dangers inherent in any family living any place in the world and in any given time in history. And it also involves all of the ingredients, ideas, and suggestions necessary to enable twentieth-century parents to be successful no matter what the circumstances.

Let's look at this Old Testament model. There are at least three major lessons for parents. It's found in Deuteronomy 6.

Experience Personal Consecration

"Hear, O Israel!"

This was the voice of Moses speaking to a multitude of people who had just completed 40 years of wilderness wanderings because of their parents' sins —parents who had engaged in unbelievable idolatry and immorality. A new generation was now camped a short distance from the Promised Land, about ready to enter in.

Moses, their leader, was reviewing the law of God. But at this moment he was interested primarily in the first commandment—the essence of the Law—and the one they had violated the most. Earlier the Lord had thundered from Mount Sinai—"I am the Lord your God . . . . You shall have no other gods before Me . . . . You shall not make for yourself an idol . . . . You shall not worship them or serve them" (Exod. 20:2–5).

Shortly after God had spoken so clearly against idolatry, the Israelites had bowed down to a golden calf, bringing the wrath of God down upon them because of their flagrant violation of His revealed word. Thus Moses reiterates—"Hear, O Israel! The Lord is our God, the Lord is one!" (Deut. 6:4). In other words, He is the absolute God! There is no other Creator or Deliverer. With this warning, Moses was exhorting the children of Israel never to turn again to the false gods of a pagan society.

But Moses' message that day included more than

what their mental and intellectual view of God should be. It also involved their emotions and their will—man's total being. Hence, Moses continued: "And you shall love the Lord your God with *all your heart* and with *all your soul* and with *all your might*. And these words, which I am commanding you today, shall be *on your heart*" (Deut. 6:5,6).

Moses was asking for total commitment and personal consecration. There was no way these people could remain true to God by mere intellectual assent to His commandments. The love he was talking about here involved *obedience*. For earlier he had said—"O Israel, you should listen and *be careful to do*" (Deut. 6:3). This kind of obedience must flow from the *heart* —the very seat of man's emotions. It must emanate from his *soul*—the very center of man's personality. It must include his *might* or his *strength*—the energy that flows from man's physical body. In short, man can only be true *to* God by becoming totally involved *with* God.

The point is clear. Earlier at Sinai the children of Israel had failed miserably as parents because they had not internalized God's word. They had only *heard* God's voice. They had not really committed themselves to Him. Their lives were still their own. They had not really taken God seriously. They had no personal consecration. When they were tempted because of their sinful desires, their insecurities and their ambitions—they reverted to their former lifestyle. The results are obvious, just as God said they would be when He first gave them the Law. In the very context of forbidding idolatry, He had said, "For, I, the Lord your God, am a jealous God, visiting the iniquity of the fathers on the children, on the third and the fourth generations of those who hate Me" (Exod. 20:5).

Emphasize Biblical Communication

Following his exhortation to personal consecration, Moses spelled out in detailed fashion how the children of Israel were to communicate to their children—obviously so the "wilderness wanderings" they had just experienced would not be repeated in the lives of their offspring. "You shall teach them diligently to your sons and shall talk of them when you *sit in your house* and when you *walk by the way* and when you *lie down* and when you *rise up*. And you shall bind them as a sign on your hand and they shall be as frontals on your forehead. And you shall write them on the doorposts of your house and on your gates" (Deut. 6:7-9).

Though these instructions no doubt include both literal and figurative elements, the children of Israel could not miss Moses' primary concern. The Word of God was to be naturally and spontaneously communicated to their children in all of their activities. When they sat down to eat, they were to thank God for providing their food. When they went for a walk, they were to praise God for a secure place to plant their feet—the Promised Land flowing with milk and honey. When they lay down to rest in the evening, they were to lift their voices in thanksgiving for their deliverance from slavery. And when they rose in the morning they were to praise God that they could face another day free from their oppressors.

And mixed with this praise and thanksgiving, they

were to teach their children the laws of God. Every day and in every way they were to integrate God's truth into their very life-style. It was to be spontaneous, natural, and constant.

There is, of course, a very obvious correlation between Moses' previous call to consecration and this charge to communication. It is only as they internalized the Word of God that they could naturally and spontaneously teach it to their children. It was only as they reflected the Scriptures in their total life-style that they could talk about it when they sat down, walked from place to place, lay down to rest, and rose up to face another day. And it was only as God's truth was "on their hearts" that their very physical presence (their "hands" and their "foreheads") and even the physical structure they called their home (the "doorposts") would reflect the will of God (see Deut. 6:8,9).

Eliminate Worldly Contamination

Israel's previous failure and downfall (bringing God's judgment) involved a renewed entanglement with the worldly system of Egypt. They even wanted to return to their position of slavery just to have more variety in their daily diet (see Num. 11:5,6). When they became impatient with Moses, even in the midst of God's mighty revelations at Sinai, they reverted to unbelievable idolatry.

Moses understood their weaknesses. He had lived with their murmurings and inconsistencies for over 40 years. Consequently, he warned them in advance: "Watch yourselves!" he said. "When the Lord your God brings you into the land . . . to give you great and splendid cities ... and houses full of all good things ... and hewn cisterns ... vineyards and olive trees ... and you shall eat and be satisfied, *then watch yourself,* lest you forget the Lord who brought you from the land of Egypt, out of the house of slavery" (Deut. 6:10-12).

I wish I could say the story ended—"And they went into Canaan, obeyed God's laws, taught their children, and experienced the full blessing of the Lord." But it didn't. In fact, the end of this story is tragic—and is still in process. The children of Israel, though given another chance by the Lord after their miserable failure at Sinai, again failed Him. And that failure resulted in divine judgment and chaos for the nation of Israel.

The book of Judges records several almost unbelievable facts about Israel once they entered the Promised Land under Joshua's leadership. In spite of repeated warnings, note what happened: "Then Joshua the son of Nun, the servant of the Lord, died .... And all that generation also were gathered to their fathers; and there arose another generation after them who did not know the Lord, nor yet the work which He had done for Israel. Then the sons of Israel did evil in the sight of the Lord, and *served the Baals,* and they forsook the Lord .... And the anger of the Lord burned against Israel" (Judg. 2:8-14).

It is difficult to comprehend such unbelief and disobedience. It is also difficult to understand how one generation can make such a profound difference in the total life-style of a nation. And yet it's true. The parents Moses addressed before they entered the land failed to do what he had said. They failed in their personal consecration and in their biblical communication to their children, and they allowed themselves and their children to become contaminated with the worldly system of Canaan. In a few short years all Israel turned away from God.

Dynamic Lessons for Twentieth-Century Parents

This Old Testament model includes relevant ideas for any family at any moment in history. In America today, as Christian parents facing in essence the same problems Israel faced, we too must align our lives with these Old Testament principles.

We must consecrate our lives to God. We can never teach our children to walk in God's ways by merely telling them that they should. We must demonstrate with our lives the reality of Christianity.

What's worse, of course, is to tell our children about God's ways, send them to church where His ways are taught, and then live a life-style contradictory to Scripture. This is doubly lethal.

Even secular psychologists recognize the power of human behavior to communicate values. J. A. Hadfield, a British psychologist who observed the growth patterns of thousands of children, made the following observation: "We see that it is by a perfectly natural process that the child develops standards of behavior and a moral sense. So that if you never taught a child one single moral maxim, he would nevertheless develop moral—or immoral—standards of right and wrong by the process of identification."[1]

In a real sense, what we are as Christians is far more important than what we say about the doctrines of Christianity. At least, what we are is foundational in creating an openness to what we say. And this is why Moses put such a strong emphasis on personal consecration and total commitment to God's Word. It is only as we, too, love the Lord our God with all our hearts and with all our souls and with all our might that our children will take seriously what we say.

We must communicate biblically. Total commitment to Christ in allowing God's Word to penetrate our total being makes it possible for us to communicate naturally and spontaneously with our children, no matter where we are or what we're doing. Formal instruction is important, but not nearly so important as natural instruction. As parents, we must be prepared to relate God's truth to the circumstances of life—as they happen. This is why Moses instructed the children of Israel to talk about the laws of God when they were sitting in their houses, walking by the way, lying down, and rising up. These are the great moments for meaningful communication—the *teachable moments.*

And notice, Moses said—"Teach them *diligently.*" This kind of constant communication takes effort. We must be alert and look for the opportunities. What better place to talk about God's creation than when walking through the woods, climbing a beautiful mountain, or driving through the countryside? What better setting to communicate God's loving care than when tucking a child to bed at night, or facing the challenges of a new day? What better place to draw attention to God's constant provisions than when sitting down to a table of delicious food? And I might add, what better opportunity to develop a deeper appreciation for the mother who has labored so diligently to prepare the meal?

Someone has said, "What we are speaks so loudly that they cannot hear what we say." This is often true, particularly from a negative point of view. But let me put it positively—"What we are speaks so loudly, they *really* hear what we say." This is what Moses was concerned about!

We must avoid worldly contamination. We cannot, of course, eliminate the world. We live in it and are surrounded by it (see 1 Cor. 5:9-11). But we need not be so negatively influenced by the world that we conform to its value system.

This was Israel's downfall. They began to worship the gods of Canaan—and also the god of materialism. When they arrived in the land and inherited material blessings galore, they soon forgot the source of these blessings. They eventually said—"We did this ourselves." And tragically, their children believed them. In other words, education works in two directions— toward God or away from God. The contamination from Canaan led this new generation away from God.

Unfortunately, the power of the negative example is more attractive than the positive one. Satan sees to that. The world offers more excitement, more immediate thrills, more personal pleasure. But the end is the way of destruction and death.

As Christian parents living in the twentieth century, we must constantly be on guard against the worldly influences of materialism and secularism. The vehicles Satan is probably using today more than any other are television, literature, movies, the secular school system, and the general life-style of the average American. And most of all, we must beware of the worldly influences that can come to our children through our own lives. Remember! It only took *one* generation to destroy Israel. Though we as parents may live with a double standard, our children will no doubt have only *one*—the world's!

Life Response

Carefully evaluate your life-style as a parent and as a Christian (the principles of parenthood are just as applicable to a Christian's witness in general) and answer the following questions as honestly as you can.

1. To what extent have I internalized God's Word? Do others (particularly my children) see that I love God with all my heart, soul, and might? Have I ever consecrated my life totally to God?

2. To what extent am I communicating biblically? Are Jesus Christ and His will for man a natural part of my conversation and life-style? Do I take advantage of opportunities—the teachable moments—to really communicate Christian truths to my children —and others?

(Note: The only way that this is natural and spontaneous is in a day-by-day dynamic relationship with Jesus Christ. Otherwise, it will be phony and superficial.)

3. Am I constantly on guard against the influence of the world—"The lust of the flesh and the lust of the eyes and the boastful pride of life" (1 John 2:16)? Am I even aware of how much I am influenced by the world?

(Note: The only criterion for evaluating the extent

the world is influencing our life is by an internalized external standard—the eternal Word of God.)

Family or Group Project

Read together Galatians 5:19-26. Here Paul contrasts the deeds of the flesh with the fruit of the Spirit. Pray together and ask God to help you "walk by the Spirit"—particularly as parents.

Footnote
1. J.A. Hadfield, *Childhood and Adolescence* (Baltimore: Penguin, 1962), p. 134.

8 DISCIPLINE
A BALANCED
PERSPECTIVE

In some respects it's dangerous (and threatening) to speak out on the subject of discipline. For one reason, there are so many conflicting voices and theories in the world today. It's all too easy to add another theory—a theory that may or may not work. And it's dangerous to "try out" theories on human beings. The results can be disastrous, since we're dealing with people's lives. It is true that a particular approach to discipline *can* affect a person for the rest of his life—either positively or negatively. Thus, it is vitally important that advice be the *right* advice!

Second, there is no subject that creates more emotional involvement and reaction, particularly on the part of parents. For some sensitive people who have already trod the torturous path of child-rearing, you can create guilt problems galore by demonstrating how many mistakes they made and how these will "forever" affect their children's personalities. For others, particularly those in the process, you can easily create frustration and insecurity, and even anger, by suggesting mid-course correction in the midst of a philosophy they're already putting into practice.

But third, because this is an emotional subject, no thinking and sensitive person can write about these issues without fear of being misinterpreted and misrepresented. When you're dealing with an emotionally laden subject, people hear you saying things you're not even saying. But write I must. For I firmly believe some things need to be said to help Christians develop a more balanced perspective on the subject of discipline.

Needed—a Fourfold Perspective!

In this chapter it's necessary to depart from the usual format; that is, the exposition of a scriptural passage or a set of verses. This is necessary because it's impossible to handle the subject of discipline adequately by considering only Scripture. We need more information than the Bible gives us—although the Bible certainly gives us many profound and basic insights—as we've already seen from Ephesians, Colossians, and Deuteronomy 6. But it also takes a broader knowledge base to really understand clearly some of the profound insights in the Bible.

Scripture, of course, for any Christian is foundational as we try to understand any particular subject. But when it comes to discipline we also need at least three other perspectives to help us interpret Scripture properly—the historical perspective, the cultural perspective, and the psychological perspective. Let's treat them in this order, ending up with the scriptural perspective as a capstone.

Historical Perspective. The "peril of the pendulum" is a persistent phenomenon in history. Whether we study education, politics, economics, or theology—various philosophies and approaches and interpretations over the years tend to swing from one extreme to the other. And views on child-rearing are no exception.

Dr. Benjamin Spock helped lead us through an era of freedom and little discipline—although he was no doubt woefully misinterpreted and blamed for things he was not guilty of. But it is true, American parents particularly reared a generation of children that often reflected in their life-style little self-control and responsible action. We must remember, however—to be fair to Dr. Spock—that there were far more influences at work in children's lives in this past 20 to 30 years than just his rather "free" view of child-rearing.

Nevertheless, the irresponsible actions of thousands of American youth led to more conservative views on discipline. Many Bible-believing Christians emphasized the fact that the Bible had taught differently all along. "If we had consulted the Scriptures rather than psychological theory," they say, "we wouldn't be in this mess."

This is basically true. And Dr. James Dobson's book, *Dare to Discipline*, was a welcome addition in the field of Christian literature. As a Christian writer, he has contributed significantly to counteracting the "peril of the pendulum."

But other Christians have gone to the other extreme. Ignoring the lessons from history and the insights from psychology, they have made the Bible teach things about discipline it really doesn't teach. But more about that later. What we must recognize at this juncture is that history says—again and again —"beware of the peril of the pendulum." Extreme views are usually not accurate—*on any subject!*

Cultural Perspective. Culture, particularly in the Western world, has probably done more than any other one thing to confuse parents in the area of child nurture and discipline. The sophistication of our society has created many and varied problems—especially for small children.

Let me illustrate. Think about how few problems children (and parents) have growing up in a society where there are no intriguing television dials to turn, no inviting electrical outlets on the wall, no colorful knobs on gas and electric stoves, no kitchen cupboards with handles at eye-level, filled with noisy equipment that appeals to the inner cravings of a two-year-old. There are no living rooms filled with sparkling vases, hanging gardens, bordered tablecloths, and numerous other untouchables. There are no ornate and multicolored "potties" which become an ego-symbol to frustrated parents who brag to neighbors and friends how soon their children were able to perform like "human beings" should—in short, not in their pants.

Speaking of pants, how comfortable it must be for children in primitive cultures who are not forced to wear twentieth-century Western diapers and tight sweaters and other assorted paraphernalia. They can "do their thing" wherever and whenever they wish, and without fear of soiling beautiful carpets. (Incidentally, some parents are more tolerant of dogs and cats than they are of their own children.)

And then there are high chairs—a real convenience *for parents*. But what a contrast for children in primitive cultures who spend the first three or four years at their mother's breast, not being forced into our "three meals a day" cultural syndrome.

And what about busy streets with fast-moving automobiles? Even 50 years ago in our own culture it was difficult for a two-year-old who wandered out on the street to get run over by a horse and buggy.

I think the point is clear. Life for children without all the conveniences and accessories that I've just described pretty much represents most biblical cultures—and many cultures today. We must face the fact that our twentieth-century Western culture has complicated life for both parents and children. And the children are the ones who must conform. In many instances, this is the root of a lot of problems in child-rearing, as well as behavioral problems in later life.

Don't misunderstand! I'm not advocating a return to a primitive life-style for children. That's impossible. However, we must *understand* these frustrations for children and *do what we* can in a "twentieth-century" way to minimize this anxiety.

Psychological Perspective. For years, psychologists have had to deal with behavioral problems in children. Without doubt, many of these problems are related to improper discipline. There is the child who is insecure because of inconsistent expectations. There is the child who is consistently angry and hostile because he has been repressed. There is the child who has learned that the only way to get the parents' attention is to get into trouble and be spanked. There is the child who has an overly sensitive conscience because the standards in the home were too high. There is the perfectionistic child whose parents are never satisfied with his behavior.

There is the sexually disturbed child—whose father or mother is too domineering and harsh. (As an adult he may want physical punishment with sex because he was severely beaten on the behind when he was a child.)

There is the child who withholds his bowel movements because he is afraid he will be spanked if he responds to his natural urges. And there is also the child who uses bowel movements—at very inappropriate times—to get even with parents who frustrate him.

I've seen all of these problems in counseling situations. All of these—and many others—can often be traced back to inappropriate approaches to child discipline. No wonder secular psychologists react against some parental "Christian" tactics. And no wonder some—especially those who do not have the true perspective of Scripture—overreact and throw the baby out with the bathwater. What is even more tragic, some secularists reject Christianity per se because Christians have inappropriately interpreted and applied Scripture in the area of child discipline.

A careful study of child psychology reveals that children, particularly in early years, have a unique "natural bent," a series of phases they go through. These phases are often misinterpreted by parents.

And cultural expectations often conflict drastically with these phases.

For example, a child in his second year—when he is just learning to really move out—enters a phase of extreme curiosity with an intense innate desire to physically explore everything in sight. Imagine what happens when this desire comes into strong conflict with all of the inviting untouchables in our sophisticated culture—especially when the main source of his conflict is a frustrated parent whose collection of untouchables is in danger of being broken, strewn all over the house, or dragged out into the middle of the street. The result is predictable. It is usually what I classify as a conflict between the parent's old nature and the child's natural bent. What's unfortunate and ironic is that we usually classify the child's innate and intense God-given desire to learn as the "old sin nature." Christians often call this strong expression to learn and this conflict with culture the "old self-will" that must be broken. That's why we've classified this phase as the "terrible twos"—which I believe is a manifestation of our contemporary sophisticated culture.

But this leads us to a very important question. What *does* the Bible teach about child discipline and about the old nature? What is a biblical point of view?

Biblical Perspective. It must be said, first of all, that the Bible definitely advocates discipline—particularly in the book of Proverbs. And the Bible also emphasizes "spankings" as a valid means of discipline. There are many verses that refer to reproving and correcting children. But I personally believe that the writer of Proverbs is seldom—if at all—referring to very young children, particularly during the first three years of life.

This may surprise you, especially since so many Christians use verses in Proverbs to support spankings of various sorts almost from the moment the child is born. There is a philosophy abroad today that equates the concept of "training" in Proverbs 22:6 with "spankings"—especially the use of the rod.

Don't misinterpret me at this juncture. What I am about to say does not mean we should never spank or even use a stick or rod of some sort—even with very young children. But the book of Proverbs does *not* teach what many Christian leaders and parents think it does.

If you will study the book carefully, looking at each verse in total context, you will note the following observations.

1. First, the book deals primarily with correcting inappropriate behavior in the life of an older boy or son who is certainly mature enough to understand some very profound instructions and symbolic language. Illustrative of this is the introductory paragraph at the very beginning of the book:

"Hear, my son, your father's instruction, and do not forsake your mother's teaching; indeed, they are a graceful wreath to your head, and ornaments about your neck. My son, if sinners entice you, do not consent. If they say, 'Come with us, let us lie in wait for blood, let us ambush the innocent without cause; let us swallow them alive like Sheol, even whole, as those who go down to the pit; we shall find all kinds of precious wealth, we shall fill our houses with spoil; throw in your lot with us, we shall all have one purse';

my son, do not walk in the way with them, keep your feet from their path; for their feet run to evil, and they hasten to shed blood" (Prov. 1:8-16).

It's obvious that Solomon is not addressing a small child, but a son who is in danger of getting involved in thievery and even murder. And this is generally true throughout the book of Proverbs. He especially warns his son against "strange women" and the "adultress" (see Prov. 2:16; 5:1-3; 6:23,24; 7:6-23; 23:26-28); he encourages him to "rejoice with the wife of your youth" rather than being "exhilarated with an adultress" (5:18,20). He warns against getting improperly involved in financial loans (6:1); he also warns against laziness when he should be working and earning a living (10:1-5); he exhorts him to accept discipline (13:1); he also instructs his son to repeat the process of discipline when he also has a son (13:24; 23:13); and he warns against assaulting his father and "driving away" his mother (19:26).

It is obvious, then, from the total context of the book of Proverbs that generally the content is directed to older children (sons particularly).

2. A second observation is that most of the verses that mention using the rod are very obviously referring to a severe form of punishment that was used in Israel for disciplining young men (and old) who were extremely rebellious and foolish in their behavior.

Note first that the Hebrew word used in Proverbs, *naghar*, and translated "child" in most English versions is rendered "young man" or "young men" or "lad" or "lads" many times in the Old Testament. Though the word is used to describe newborns on occasions, its predominant use refers to older children or youth—particularly older boys. In view of the general and specific contexts in Proverbs, it is a valid question, at least, to ask why the word is translated "child" in the book of Proverbs rather than "young man" or "lad."

To be fair, however, it must be noted that it is impossible to demonstrate conclusively what age level the Hebrew word translated "child" in most versions refers to in Proverbs. We can only speculate on the basis of the overall content of the book, which definitely infers that in most situations the writer had older children in view.

Note second that the verses that mention specifically the use of the rod for discipline (or imply the use of the rod) also imply from the context very *severe* discipline—and for very serious misdemeanors.

> 10:13—"On the lips of the discerning, wisdom is found, but a *rod* is for the back of him who lacks understanding."
>
> 13:24—"He who spares his rod hates his son, but he who loves him disciplines him *diligently.*"
>
> 17:10—"A rebuke goes deeper into one who has understanding than *a hundred blows* into a fool."
>
> 18:6—"A fool's lips bring strife, and his mouth calls for *blows.*"
>
> 19:29—"Judgments are prepared for scoffers, and *blows for the back* of fools."
>
> 20:30—"Stripes that *wound* scour away evil, and strokes reach the innermost parts."

22:15—"Foolishness is bound up in the heart of a child; the rod of discipline will remove it far from him."

23:13,14—"Do not hold back discipline from the child, although you *beat* him with the rod, he will *not die.* You shall *beat* him with the rod, and deliver his soul from Sheol."

26:3—"A whip is for the horse, a bridle for the donkey, and a rod for the back of fools."

29:15—"The rod and reproof give wisdom, but a child who gets his own way brings shame to his mother."

To understand thoroughly the purpose and use of the rod in Israel, we need a broader cultural and scriptural view. Philip G. Baldensperger, who researched this subject years ago, gave us some very helpful insights. He said: "There are many kinds of sticks, rods, and staves which Orientals always have in their hands . . . . The first is . . . a common stick of oak, about three to three and a half feet in length, which is carried in the hand or under the arm . . . . The government officials, superior officers, tax-gatherers, and school masters used this short rod to threaten and, if necessary, to beat their inferiors, whoever they may be. A good stick of this kind is supposed to have forty knots. One associates with this the Hebrew *sebet,* with which the Israelite chastised his servant (Exod. 21:20, compare also Prov. 10:13)."[1]

If this is a true description of the rod in the Old Testament (and it probably comes close), we can see

117

that it was an instrument that was used as a severe form of discipline and punishment. And this was also true in Israel—and by the commandment of God. Note the law of God as given in Deuteronomy 25: "If there is a dispute between men and they go to court, and the judges decide their case, and they justify the righteous and condemn the wicked, then it shall be if the wicked man deserves to be *beaten*, the judge shall make him *lie down* and *be beaten* in his presence with the number of *stripes* according to his guilt. He may *beat him forty times* but no more, lest he beat him with many more stripes than these, and your brother be degraded in your eyes" (vv. 1-3).

This practice was still being carried on in New Testament days by both Gentiles and Jews. In Philippi, Paul and Silas were disrobed by the Romans and "beaten with rods" (Acts 16:22, *NASB*). And in Paul's letter to the Corinthians, he reported: "Five times I received from the Jews thirty-nine lashes" (2 Cor. 11:24).

The rod, then (which is mentioned in the Bible and referred to the most in Proverbs) was used as a means of disciplining what appeared to be very inappropriate and wicked behavior. The extreme form of punishment for certain crimes in Israel, of course, was stoning (for example, see Lev. 24:13,14). It appears that the use of the rod was a form of punishment short of death. Thus we read in Proverbs that in such cases an Israelite father should not fear to beat his son in this way for such wicked behavior because "he will not die." Rather, Solomon wrote, to "beat . . . with the rod" will help to "deliver his soul from Sheol" (Prov. 23:13,14).

We must conclude that to apply these verses in Proverbs to child-rearing and discipline with very small children, is certainly not what Solomon had in mind. Rather, it seems he was referring to a form of punishment against various crimes that were committed in the Hebrew society. To use these verses to develop a philosophy of child-rearing and discipline in the home has created some unusual behavioral problems in children—and often brings unfortunate criticism from non-Christian counselors who know from experience that this is not an appropriate approach.

The Old Nature—What Is It?

Another serious misrepresentation and misapplication of Scripture is always to treat natural tendencies in children as a manifestation of the old sin nature. Again, there is no question about what the Bible teaches in this area. All children are born with a sinful nature. But what is this nature? How does it manifest itself? And when?

Dr. Charles Ryrie defines the old nature clearly: "It is far better to define nature in terms of a capacity. Thus the old nature of the flesh is that capacity which all men have to serve and please self. Or, one might say that it is the capacity to leave God out of one's life. It would not be inclusive enough to define the sin nature in terms of a capacity to do evil, because it is more than that. There are many things which are not necessarily in themselves evil, but which stem from the old nature. They simply are things which leave God out. The flesh, then, is that old capacity which all men have to live lives which exclude God. In the

Christian, that flesh is the same capacity to leave God out of his life and actions."[2]

The old nature is a capacity—the capacity that is soon affected by the content of life. As a child matures and develops, this capacity is greatly affected by environmental conditions. If the child is in an environment that is characterized by Christian attitudes, he tends to take on the same characteristics—even apart from conversion. If he is in an atmosphere that is characterized by non-Christian attitudes he tends to take on those characteristics.

Evangelical Christians frequently make the mistake of classifying the old nature of a two-year-old as a full-blown manifestation of sin. We do this because we see the child through adult eyes (our own adult perspective). We often interpret the biblical references to the degenerative manifestation of the sin nature in adult people as being applicable to very small children—from birth. Manifestations of anger, for example, from the child is classified in the same category as if it were an adult losing his temper. Manifestations of self-centeredness are often classified as the same type of manifestation as may also appear in adults. Interest and curiosity in his sexual nature is sometimes classified as a manifestation of the same thing we see in sinning adults. To some Christians, these characteristics in a child are proof positive that he is expressing sinful actions—and to get rid of them, we must "drive them out of him." And here, of course, we quote Proverbs 22:15—"Foolishness is bound up in the heart of a child; the rod of discipline will remove it far from him." The problem, of course, is we do not define "foolishness" as does the author of the book of Proverbs. It is clear from the context that the "foolishness" he is talking about involves the degenerative activities that often characterize young men and which are described in the book of Proverbs (note Prov. 26, which gives a very explicit description of "foolish" behavior).

The Natural Bent—What Is It?

Psychologists have noted for a long time that children pass through certain phases—particularly in their early years. In order to understand the natural bent, we *must* understand these phases.

The exploratory phase (ages one and two.) One of the most significant is the exploratory phase at age two, which in our culture gets a child into serious trouble. These strong urges come into direct conflict with cultural demands. When a child is overly restricted, one of two things happens. Either he becomes a very quiet and cooperative and non-investigative personality; or he becomes extremely hostile and anxious, creating persistent discipline problems. The former child seems to have less physical and emotional energy from birth. The latter is loaded with it.

Neither response is healthy. The child with low motivation needs to be encouraged toward exploration. The child with lots of energy needs to be channeled. But his exploratory desires need to be developed even more. In later life it will be one of his greatest assets in doing great exploits for God. This is why we must channel and develop the will to explore—not "break" it.

The imitation phase (ages one and two). Another

natural phase is the imitation phase. The natural capacity to imitate comes into full force between one and two years of age. What the child imitates comes from his environment. It appears to be a subconscious process, is unrelated to his power to reason, and is far more effective than verbal teaching.

This natural phase, of course, also gets him into serious trouble in our culture. Between one and two he wants to do everything his mother and father do. When mother pulls pans out of the cupboard, he wants to do the same thing. When daddy turns on the television, he wants to imitate daddy's behavior. And, of course, it's just with this type of action that he is confronted with a slap on the hand or a verbal no that he soon learns will take on more serious connotations. Here again the child is caught between his natural innate desire to imitate and to explore, and the fact that he cannot.

But there is also the positive side to this. As parents, we must be living models of Jesus Christ with a child this age. The child naturally and spontaneously imitates our behavior. He reflects either our bad habits or our good habits. If we act in impatient ways, he reflects impatience. If we are selfish, he reflects selfishness. If we are insecure, he reflects insecurity. If we constantly strike out at him, he learns to strike back.

This does not mean we should never spank a child between the ages of one and two. It is sometimes necessary just to keep him from hurting himself and others. But wise parents who understand his exploratory and imitation phases will work with these phases and structure his environment so that the need for confrontations and spankings are minimized.

Identification (ages two and three). This is a more advanced stage in the child's development. During this period the child tends to take on the personality of a parent. This tendency is most noticeable in a three-year-old.

Since a child most normally identifies with those he loves and admires, it is important for parents and teachers to establish a relationship with children that reflects security and a feeling of comfortableness. The more a child is attracted to you, the more he will want to be like you.

Organization of the personality (ages three and four). Another significant phase in a child is the organization of his personality about age four. For the first time in his life he becomes truly aware of himself, he can engage in healthy or unhealthy self-criticism, and he has the capacity for significant self-control in most areas of his life. He has the ability to reason things through and can understand and comprehend concepts and ideas.

Interestingly, this is the time many children really understand the gospel for the first time, recognize that they are sinners by nature, and begin to experience true duality in their personality—a conscious pull toward sinful actions and, on the other hand, a desire to please God.

From a biblical point of view, this is an extremely important age. It is at this time that the biblical doctrine regarding the old nature becomes significant. The Adamic capacity (which has been there since birth) begins to become a strong force in the child's life—a force which the child does not understand, but one which Christian parents and teachers *must* understand.

Proverbs and the Natural Bent

Interestingly, Proverbs also says something about the *natural bent*, and perhaps at this point, the word "child" may be an appropriate translation. However, it may also refer to a young man, for even adolescent children go through natural phases that must be recognized by parents.

Proverbs 22:6 reads: "Train up a child in the way he should go, even when he is old he will not depart from it."

Here again, many Christians have misinterpreted this verse. As I mentioned earlier, some Christians believe that the primary meaning of this verse is the use of a rod in discipline. But Delitzsch appropriately translates it: "Give to the child instruction conformable to his way; so he will not, when he becomes old, depart from it." Or as he says in his commentary on this verse, "The instruction of youth, the education of youth, ought to be conformed to the *nature* of youth; the matter of instruction, the manner of instruction, ought to regulate itself according to the stage of life, and its peculiarities; the method ought to be arranged according to the degree development which the mental and bodily life of the youth has arrived at."[3]

This verse, of course, is speaking clearly of the natural bent, the phases of natural development as created by God. If we cooperate with this natural development, we will have good results. If we work against it, we will experience negative results.

Disciplining Children the First Three Years

1. In view of the obvious natural bent of the child in the first three years, particularly his desire to explore, and in view of cultural obstacles that get him into trouble, Christian parents should do all they can to remove these barriers so a child is not in constant tension with his environment. This is particularly true for a child between one and two-and-a-half years of age.

2. Christian parents should make use of the natural tendency to imitate and identify at age two, rather than work against it. For example, avoid creating situations where you have to demonstrate negative behavior. And when a child wants to imitate your day-to-day behavior (cooking, washing the car, gardening) give him opportunity to participate—even to help you.

3. Minimize the times you have to say no. Reserve them for the *must* situations. One psychologist believes that nine out of ten times when a parent says no, he wouldn't have if he were thinking ahead in the situation. Remember, too, that saying no can become a habit for a parent and when it does, it often becomes a meaningless word to the child.

4. Don't get in a hurry to wean a child away from the breast, a bottle, or a pacifier. Children in biblical times nursed at the breast until they were three, which, of course, is not culturally acceptable today. But this practice certainly provided tremendous feelings of security for the child. Since in our culture we emphasize early weaning, we must be sensitive to substitute experiences that help the child to develop the security that he needs.

5. Don't push a child in toilet-training. Allow the natural process of imitation and identification to work for you. Remember a child wants to be like you. Set a good example. Don't be so affected by our present culture that you always have to close the bathroom door on a little child. Mothers should set the example for little girls and fathers for little boys.

And remember! The average age a child should be toilet-trained is around three. Don't rush it. And by all means, don't get ego-involved.

6. Don't view training a child as synonymous with spanking him. This theory comes out of a false interpretation of the use of the rod in Proverbs. You will have occasions when you will have to spank, even in the very early years, but if you equate spanking with training you're going to use it as a focal means rather than as something that is necessary only as a final solution.

7. Remember that spankings become more effective when a child can understand *why* he is being spanked. And this ability becomes most obvious during age three and particularly four. Before this time, a spanking is primarily a conditioning technique— that is, gaining a response from the child because he wants to avoid physical or emotional pain.

(Conditioning is sometimes necessary—particularly in our culture. But attempt to minimize it. If you try to consider the child's nature and viewpoint in the matter, you'll find you *can* minimize these occasions —and with significant results.)

8. Treat a child the way you like to be treated. Don't expect more from him than you do of yourself. Realize that when he gets tired, his frustration level

is far lower than yours is. Remember that when he gets hungry, his drives are even more intense than yours are. Remember that his nervous system, too, is generally far more sensitive than yours. When you're tempted to get upset with him when he is out of sorts, stop and think what you are like when you are out of sorts—and what's causing it.

9. Look for symptoms of over-discipline and over-restrictive behavior. The following will help you isolate these problems, and enable you to make some mid-course corrections:

 a. A withdrawn and overly quiet child

 b. A very aggressive and angry child—one who is always striking back or striking out at others

 c. An oversensitive and fearful child

 d. A child who is never satisfied with his accomplishments, a perfectionist

 e. Anger turned inward upon himself—a desire to die

 f. A very uncooperative child—particularly at age three or four

 g. A sneaky child

 h. A child who is constantly misbehaving to get attention

(All of these symptoms are also seen in normal day-to-day behavior. However, in a child who has been over-restricted, such behaviors are quite persistent.)

Disciplining Children Ages Three and Over

1. Most children need periodic spankings as they grow and develop. However, if you have to spank a

child with a degree of regularity without gaining results, chances are you are dealing with a child who is misbehaving because of over-restriction in the very early years. He may also be expressing a need for attention. It may be that he only got attention in the early years when he did something to irritate you. If this is true, you'll need to take another tactic—perhaps even ignoring his negative behavior (within reason) and complimenting him for his positive behavior.

It is also true, however, that some children who develop negative behavior because of poor disciplinary tactics in the early years can only be corrected through persistent and consistent spankings. However, if you do not get results over a relatively brief period of time, you'd better check to see if you're making the problem worse. Seek help from a competent counselor.

2. Older children (particularly ages six to nine) who are insecure, angry, or emotionally disturbed will consistently try to irritate parents—to get even. At this point you may need to ignore this kind of behavior (within reason) and above all, not get emotionally involved.

3. Be consistent in your discipline. But make sure you're realistic in your threats. Don't say "I'll spank you if you do that again" when the "punishment" doesn't match the "crime." Think before you threaten a child. Then carry through on what you say—unless you're totally unreasonable in what you have demanded. Remember: Inconsistent discipline creates real insecurity in a child. And insecurity usually results in anger.

4. With teenagers, discuss the matters that are bothering you, and if possible work out feasible solutions together as well as disciplinary action. If there is no cooperation, then think through reasonable expectations and lay down the law. If there is violation, stick to your threats.

(In our culture, most teenagers respond to discipline that is not physical.)

5. Remember, the Proverbs deal with extreme behavior and also set forth a cultural form for punishment that was uniquely related to the civil laws governing Israel's society. Most Christian parents will never have to resort to these extreme forms of punishment if they follow the principles of Christianity and reflect Jesus Christ in their total life-style.

Footnotes

1. Philip G. Baldensperger, "The Immovable East," *Palestine Exploration Fund Quarterly* (January, 1905), pp. 33,34.
2. Charles C. Ryrie, *Balancing the Christian Life* (Chicago: Moody Press, 1969), pp. 34,35).
3. Carl F. Keil and Franz Delitzsch, *Proverbs, Ecclesiastes, Song of Solomon* (vol. 6) (Grand Rapids: William B. Eerdmans Publishing Co., 1971), pp. 86,87.

9 UNEQUALLY YOKED
SOME BIBLICAL GUIDELINES

The Bible gives us a prescription for an ideal marriage and family life—as much as this is possible in a world contaminated by sin. But life generally is not filled with ideal situations. For example, Jane is married to a man who is not a Christian. She's a new Christian herself and her husband thinks she's flipped out. In fact, he's pretty threatened by the whole episode, especially since she talks about her new Christian friends.

John's situation is different. He has been a Christian for years—ever since he was six years old. He grew up in a good Christian home. And he had good Bible teaching in his church. Furthermore, he heard numerous Sunday School lessons and sermons on the problem of marrying a person who is not a Christian.

He had even memorized the verse from Corinthians which says—"Do not be yoked together with unbelievers" (2 Cor. 6:14).

But he met a nice girl in high school, developed a good relationship, and eventually married her—with the hope, of course, that she'd soon become a Christian, too. But she never has. In fact, she never goes to church with him, opposes reading the Bible with the children, and, in general, resents any conversation about spiritual issues. Needless to say, John's not too happy with his marriage.

Joan's situation is different still. Her husband professes to be a Christian. But he shows little interest in spiritual things. He never takes the lead spiritually, never prays with the family, never reads the Bible—alone or with the family—never encourages regular church attendance. He doesn't oppose Joan's involvement. He's just neutral. No interest, no enthusiasm—just plain neutral.

And then there's Bob. He's a Christian and his wife isn't. Because of his faith in Christ and involvement in Christian activities, she wants a divorce—and as soon as possible. Says she—"We've nothing in common any more! Let's each start over—with someone else." Bob loves his wife, and he's heartbroken about the situation.

These, and many other similar situations, exist with an infinite variety of problems which keep husband-and-wife relationships and family life from being ideal. Added to these sample cases are countless Christian couples who are merely living together, having long since lost their feelings of attraction to each other and the excitement of life. In many instances, they are simply staying together "for the children's sake"—or because they believe it's wrong to separate or get a divorce.

What can people do under these circumstances? Does the Bible offer any solutions? Fortunately, it does! And we've already looked at the most basic answers. In marriage—to be able to experience God's ideal while on earth—there must be reciprocal love and respect. It's a two-way street. Husbands must love as Christ loved. And wives must submit as the Church is to submit to Christ. When this process is reciprocal and mutual, it leads to deeper love and respect. But when it is one-sided, when one partner is selfish and the other unselfish, when one partner is always giving and the other is always getting, there will be inevitable deterioration in the relationship. Even the strongest Christian will eventually crumble under prolonged stress of this nature.

But there are some scriptural principles that will often help Christians break through some of these difficult barriers and help solve what appear to be almost insurmountable problems.

A Biblical Strategy

The apostle Peter gave some specific instructions to Christians who were married to non-Christian mates. His primary emphasis constitutes "visual" rather than "verbal" witness. He spoke first to women: "Wives, in the same way be submissive to your husbands so that, if any of them do not believe the word, they may be won over *without talk by the behavior of their wives*" (1 Pet. 3:1).

Peter then spelled out clearly what this behavior

entailed. It should involve "purity" and "reverence"; that is, a life of moral purity (in short, being faithful sexually). The wife should live a life that reflects godly fear. And though Peter does not say a woman shouldn't make herself beautiful on the outside, he emphasized that inner beauty (a gentle and quiet spirit) constitutes the qualities that really please both God and man. This, said Peter, may attract her non-Christian husband to Jesus Christ.

There's a valuable lesson here for both men and women. To men, external beauty (what Peter classifies as "outward adornment, such as braided hair and the wearing of gold jewelry and fine clothes," v. 3) *is* attractive and appealing. But it can be very deceptive. Good marriages are not built and sustained on externals. A woman may catch a man's eye with her outward beauty, but if she's going to really hold his attention, it's what's on the inside that really counts. The world, in its advertising schemes, has reversed this concept—but only because they're operating with a very superficial and existential philosophy. They are only thinking of the immediate moment, the one-night stand, the fun-and-games approach to life, which is totally removed from reality.

Unfortunately—and it's not easy to admit—most of us as men can be easily deceived. We're so motivated by outward beauty that we lose sight of reality. We think existentially. We can be very superficial and selfish in a relationship with a woman. That's why so many men use women—"love 'em and leave 'em."

But down deep, that's not what a man wants, nor is it what impresses him. Whether he is a Christian or a non-Christian, spiritual or carnal, he is ultimately attracted to "the *unfading beauty* of a gentle and quiet spirit" (1 Pet. 3:4).

You see, external beauty *is* attractive; it *is* appealing; it does attract initial attention. And it may be a primary factor in getting a man to the altar. But it will never sustain a marriage. In fact, there is ultimately nothing more repulsive and deadening to a man's inner feelings than a woman who is beautiful on the outside and ugly on the inside. The impact of external beauty quickly fades away when internal beauty is missing.

But what constitutes inner beauty? What does Peter mean by a "gentle and quiet spirit"? Perhaps it can best be illustrated by what it isn't. A woman who always nags doesn't fit the picture Peter is painting. A woman who has a loud, raucous voice—who screams at the kids and her husband—doesn't fit the picture either. A female voice that is harsh and cutting can literally destroy a relationship—with both her husband and her children. A woman who puts her husband down, embarrasses him in public, and is insensitive to his self-image can ruin a potentially good marriage.

I've known men who have been so turned off by this kind of behavior that they don't want to come home from work at night. They take their day off and leave town. They do everything they can to avoid being around their wives. They don't communicate about anything—except when it's absolutely necessary. Unless the man has very high morals and standards, he is easy prey for another woman—especially someone who is sensitive, who has learned to listen, and who demonstrates understanding. What's ironic (and pathetic) is that this kind of behavior from a husband makes an insensitive woman very insecure, so that she screams all the louder, and the cycle is perpetuated.

But men, this is a two-way street. Though Peter talked first to New Testament wives who were married to unsaved husbands, he quickly directed some instructions to men—"Husbands," he wrote, "*in the same way* be considerate as you live with your wives" (1 Pet. 3:7). In other words, a Christian husband will never win his unsaved wife to Christ by being an insensitive, demanding, and selfish husband. He must love her as Christ loved the Church—even though she is not a Christian. After all, this is what Christ did for us. When we were yet sinners He died for us (see Rom. 5:8).

Note the larger context in which Peter's exhortation to wives and husbands occurs. Earlier in his letter he had said, "Live such good lives among the pagans that, though they accuse you of doing wrong, they may see your good deeds and glorify God on the day he visits us" (1 Pet. 2:12). And these pagans, Peter went on to say, include kings (2:13), governors (2:14), slave masters (2:18), *and* non-Christian mates (3:1-7).

When it seems almost impossible to face the suffering and heartache involved, Peter reminded these New Testament Christians to think about Jesus Christ—"But if you suffer for doing good and you endure it, this is commendable before God. To this you were called, because Christ suffered for you, leaving you an *example*, that you should follow in his steps. 'He committed no sin, and no deceit was found in his mouth.' When they hurled their insults at him, he did not retaliate; when he suffered, he made no threats. Instead, he entrusted himself to him who judges justly. He himself bore our sins in his body on the cross, so that we might die to sins and live for righteousness; by his wounds you have been healed. For you were like sheep going astray, but now you have returned to the Shepherd and Overseer of your souls" (1 Pet. 2:20-25).

Following this descriptive, Christ-centered argument for being submissive to non-Christian authority figures, he turned immediately to the marriage relationship and said: "Wives, *in the same way* be submissive to your husbands so that, if any of them do not believe the word, they may be won over without talk by the behavior of their wives" (1 Pet. 3:1). Jesus Christ, then, is our supreme example in our relationship to non-Christians—even a non-Christian mate.

What, then, is the best approach for a Christian woman to attempt to win her non-Christian husband to Jesus Christ? In essence, Peter is saying "be a good wife"—the same as if you were married to a Christian. Love him! Be submissive to him! Honor him! Respect him! Be loyal to him! Demonstrate a gentle and quiet spirit. Follow the example of godly women of old. "For this is the way the holy women of the past who put their hope in God used to make themselves beautiful. They were submissive to their own husbands, like Sarah, who obeyed Abraham and called him her master. You are her daughters if you do what is right and do not give way to fear" (1 Pet. 3:5,6).

Sometimes it is easy for a woman in certain circumstances to become fearful and insecure in a relationship involving a non-Christian mate. This was particularly true in the New Testament culture. In some instances, a woman's very life was in danger. A disobedient wife could be disposed of rather quickly —and not merely by asking her to leave. In some instances, it might be a matter of life and death.

But there are circumstances that are similar in the twentieth century. And Peter's instructions still stand. Though cultural factors may vary, the principle still endures and applies. And if *any* approach will work, this will. Hard indeed is the heart of a man (or woman) who will not respond to the unconditional love of Christ when it is truly and consistently demonstrated—even in the midst of a relationship that is not reciprocal.

Some Twentieth-Century Questions

It's one thing to talk about biblical principles and Christian idealism, but it's another thing to work through the nitty-gritty problems of day-to-day living. And in some instances, difficult questions emerge. Solutions are hard to come by. But we can face at least some of them satisfactorily.

1. What if there is no response to the approach specified by Peter? In fact, what if the problem gets worse?

First, we must remember that God has not *guaranteed* a particular response—either that the unsaved mate will come to Christ or that there will be more positive attitudes and behavior. However, *most* people (if they are human at all and in their right

138

mind) *will* eventually respond in more positive ways to Christlike behavior in any relationship. As Solomon reminds us in Proverbs: "A gentle answer turns away wrath, but a harsh word stirs up anger" (Prov. 15:1).

Regarding the matter getting worse, this sometimes happens. In fact, some people are so insecure, selfish, and just plain ornery, that they'll add additional pressures just to test a person's motives. In other words, to see if all of this kind and gracious behavior is the real thing. So be prepared! It *might* get worse before it gets better.

2. What if there seems to be no response whatever? How long should a Christian put up with this kind of situation?

First of all, if there's no response, a Christian mate should make sure he (or she) is truly responding in a Christlike way. Some people have a strange view of what Christlikeness is. They are "sweet for a day"— or a week—and then revert to their old habits. And then they wonder why the other person is not responding. An unbeliever is impressed with consistent Christian attitudes—not sporadic bursts of "gentleness" and "kindness." In fact, inconsistency can be very confusing.

You'll need to check yourself! Use the following checklist. As much as is humanly possible, have you, with God's help, eliminated these negative characteristics from your marital and family life-style? Have you sought the Lord in prayer, asking Him to help you become His kind of person? Are you studying the Scriptures regularly and fellowshipping with God's people, seeking and getting the encouragement you need to be a consistent Christian?

A Christian Wife's Checklist. The following statements are designed to help you evaluate your attitudes and actions toward your non-Christian husband:

- ☐ I do not nag my unsaved husband.
- ☐ I do not show jealousy toward his friends or his job.
- ☐ I do not complain about his schedule.
- ☐ I do not reveal lack of trust.
- ☐ I do not embarrass him in public.
- ☐ I do not respond to him with bitterness or rancor in my voice.
- ☐ I do not run him down before others.
- ☐ I do not shout or scream at him.
- ☐ I do not demand my own way.
- ☐ I do not argue with him.
- ☐ I do not allow my friends or activities to interfere with time I need to meet his needs.
- ☐ I keep our house clean and neat.
- ☐ I try to make our home a comfortable place for him to live.
- ☐ I'm available to meet his sexual needs.
- ☐ I do not put him down publicly or privately.
- ☐ I keep myself attractive physically.
- ☐ I do not spend money carelessly or foolishly.
- ☐ I avoid talking to him about my wonderful Christian friends.
- ☐ I do not allow others to interfere with my relationship with my husband and family.

A Christian husband's checklist. The following statements are designed to help you evaluate your attitudes and actions toward your non-Christian wife:

☐ I provide sufficient income for her to meet household and personal expenses.

☐ I trust her to do a good job in the home.

☐ I plan my schedule so I can spend time with her.

☐ I am courteous and always treat her like a lady.

☐ I keep myself physically attractive.

☐ I do what I can to let her know she is frequently in my thoughts.

☐ I listen to her complaints without being threatened.

☐ I communicate regularly what I'm doing, where I'm going, and what my daily schedule involves.

☐ I am on time for meals, and if there are emergencies, I call ahead of time.

☐ I become involved with the children.

☐ I try to help my wife around the house, caring for jobs that only a man can do efficiently.

☐ I find opportunities for her to get away from the home and the routine—alone or with her friends.

☐ I carve out time for just the two of us to be alone.

☐ I do not show jealousy toward her friends.

☐ I don't shout at her, abuse her, or make unreasonable demands upon her.

☐ I don't use force as a means to get my own way.

☐ I avoid talking a lot to her about other women —especially wonderful Christian women.

3. I've done all these things, but I still have an unbearable situation. Now what?

First, define "unbearable." Some people rationalize, and because they are not "happy," they classify their situation as "unbearable." An unbearable situation is one where we can no longer cope. We cannot tolerate it physically, emotionally, or spiritually.

In this case, seek help from other mature Christians, specifically the elders of the church. It is their responsibility to assist you—to help you evaluate your situation. In some instances, it *is* an impossible situation. Some people are so sick spiritually and psychologically they will literally destroy another individual no matter what you do. In this case, the non-Christian (or Christian) needs to be lovingly confronted with his inappropriate response. But remember, you must be prepared for the consequences of such action.

4. What if my unsaved mate wants to leave—to get a divorce?

Paul answers this question very specifically in his first letter to the Corinthian Christians: "If any brother has a wife who is not a believer and she is willing to live with him, he must not divorce her. And if a woman has a husband who is not a believer and he is willing to live with her, she must not divorce him. For the unbelieving husband has been sanctified through his wife, and the unbelieving wife has been sanctified through her husband. Otherwise your children would be 'unclean,' but as it is, they are holy. But if the unbeliever leaves, let him do so. A believing man or woman is not bound in such circumstances; God has called us to live in peace" (1 Cor. 7:12-15).

A Final Word

The preceding checklists, of course, are designed

for Christians married to non-Christians. But they certainly apply to Christians who are also married to Christians. Two people who truly attempt to apply these guidelines on a consistent basis will discover unusual happiness and harmony in marriage.

But there is another situation that needs special attention. What if both are Christians, but one partner is spiritual and the other is carnal—leading to unusual stress and difficulty in the home? Two suggestions. First, attempt to live the same way you would if you were living with a non-Christian mate. But second, if there are no results over a reasonable period of time, you should seek help from the elders of the church, for this is a matter calling for church discipline. A Christian who is part of a local body of believers, and who is living in consistent sin (and mistreating a Christian mate is sin), should be lovingly but directly confronted with that sin (see Gal. 6:1, 2).

Family or Group Project

As a Christian couple, evaluate each other by using the two checklists. Check those items where you feel your mate could improve significantly. Then sensitively share *why* and *how* this improvement could take place.

If you are yet single, the greatest lesson that comes from this passage of Scripture in 1 Peter is what Paul wrote to the Corinthians—"do not be yoked together with unbelievers" (2 Cor. 6:14).

10 THE SINGLE PARENT
SOME BIBLICAL GUIDELINES

Jean is divorced. She has three children, lives in a rented apartment, and works forty hours a week as a receptionist in a downtown office complex. Her child-support is minimal, but she manages to get by. When she has paid all her bills, she's fortunate if she has enough left for a little family entertainment, but at least she has been able to care for the basic needs of her family. And since she has become a Christian she has been setting aside a certain percentage of the monthly income for the Lord's work—a new experience for Jean. She has been amazed how God has blessed her for this step of faith.

Jean became a Christian a year ago. She was divorced a couple of years before that when her former husband deserted her and the family for another woman. Since coming to know Christ as her personal Saviour, she has found new hope. She was a lonely and bitter person before she became a Christian. And though she still struggles with the problems of the past—and the present—she now has a new outlook on life. It's a pretty rough road sometimes, being both mother and father to her children, but she's determined to face her problems with her chin up. Her favorite verse is Philippians 4:13—"I can do everything through him who gives me strength." She quotes it to herself often—because often she doesn't feel she can face another day. But she always has.

This true-to-life story represents an increasing number of people—both men and women—who face life as single parents. As divorce rates continue to skyrocket in the American culture, so do the number of situations where one parent or the other is left to bring up children, to make a living, and to face alone what God intended to be a dual leadership responsibility.

What can be said, from a Christian point of view, to encourage these people? How can all of us as members of Christ's body minister to the single parent? What must they do to face their problems responsibly? These are questions we must all face as Christians.

A Biblical Perspective

The Bible is filled with injunctions and illustrations regarding the responsibility every member of Christ's body has for all others. Listen to Paul: "The body is a unit, though it is made up of many parts; and though all its parts are many, they form one body .... The eye cannot say to the hand, 'I don't need you!' And the head cannot say to the feet, 'I don't need you!' On the contrary, those parts of the body that seem to be weaker are indispensable, and the parts that we think are less honorable we treat with special honor. And the parts that are unpresentable are treated with special modesty, while our presentable parts need no special treatment. But God has combined the members of the body and has given greater honor to the parts that lacked it, so that there should be no division in the body, but that its parts should have equal concern for each other. If one part suffers, every part suffers with it; if one part is honored, every part rejoices with it" (1 Cor. 12:12,21-26).

The point, of course, is clear. We're all members of Christ's body—including the single parent. But there are two illustrations in Scripture that provide special encouragement for single parents—and all Christians. Though we cannot be sure of all the details, there is sufficient information in these biblical accounts to provide motivation and guidelines for both single parents and other members of Christ's body whose lives touch people who *are* single parents.

Lydia, a dealer in purple cloth (Acts 16:11-15). Lydia was Paul's first convert in Philippi. She was a businesswoman, "a dealer in purple cloth from the city of Thyatira" (Acts 16:14). Paul met her at a prayer meeting, on a river bank outside the city of Philippi. Though she was a religious woman who worshiped God, she was not yet a Christian. But when she heard Paul share the good news about salvation, she welcomed Christ into her life to be her personal Saviour. We read: "The Lord opened her heart to respond to Paul's message" (16:14).

We are told very little about Lydia's family situation. We can only speculate. Chances are that she appears in Scripture as a single parent. It seems obvious that she had a family—a family that also responded to the gospel, because Luke records that "she and the members of her household were baptized" (v. 15).

Following her conversion and the conversion of the members of her household, she invited Paul and his traveling companions to come and stay in her house. In fact, she insisted. "If you consider me a believer in the Lord," she said, "come and stay at my house." And we read further—"She persuaded us" (v. 15). And, as we might expect, Paul and his fellow workers accepted her invitation. In fact, some believe that Lydia's home may have been the first meeting place for the church at Philippi.

If Lydia was indeed an example of a single parent in Scripture—and chances are she was—we can make several very significant observations.

First, she was a successful businesswoman—a dealer in purple cloth. She did not allow her status in life to keep her from functioning as a responsible person. She no doubt bore the sole responsibility for providing for her family.

Second, she evidently had a strong influence on her children and others in her household. They, too, responded to the gospel. As a woman, she had the same influence that most fathers had in first-century households. She did not allow the absence of a man to keep her from functioning in such a way that her children would respect her and follow her example when making their own decisions.

Third, she immediately demonstrated Christian hospitality, opening her home to Paul and his fellow-missionaries. Again, she did not allow her status in life to keep her from being a servant of the Lord.

Fourth, even before she became a Christian, her heart was turned toward God. She desired to put Him first in her life. And when she became a Christian, there was no question about her priorities.

All of this adds up to the fact that Lydia did not allow a male-dominated culture to keep her from being a successful single parent. She arranged her priorities and proceeded to do what had to be done. And God honored her efforts, even allowing her to become the first convert to Christianity in the whole geographical area in which she lived.

Eunice, Timothy's mother (Acts 16:1; 2 Timothy 1:5; 3:14,15). Eunice represents a much different family situation. In a sense, she was a "single parent" only in that she bore the major responsibility for the spiritual nurture of her young son, Timothy. Her husband was probably not a Christian. In the book of Acts we read that she "was a Jewess and a believer," but her husband "was a Greek" (16:1).

This example also represents numerous families today. Many women have come to know Christ personally while their husbands continue in an unbelieving state. And, obviously, no matter how good a husband and father he might be, the primary responsibility for spiritual nurture will fall upon his Christian mate.

This is what happened in Timothy's home. His mother performed her spiritual task well. She was a godly woman, a woman of faith (see 2 Tim. 1:5). And Paul was certainly referring to her faithfulness in nurturing her young son when he later wrote to Timothy, then a grown man—"But as for you, continue in what you have learned and have become convinced of, because you know those from whom you learned it, and how *from infancy* you have known the holy Scriptures, which are able to make you wise for salvation through faith in Christ Jesus" (2 Tim. 3:14,15).

It is true that God's ideal calls for both parents to be involved in Christian nurture, especially the father (see Eph. 6:4). But this is not always possible, as we see from this biblical example. Eunice demonstrates clearly that it *is* possible to bring up children "in the training and instruction of the Lord," even though one parent is not a Christian.

Obviously, some situations are far more difficult, especially if a non-Christian mate is hostile toward God and His Son, Jesus Christ.

Some Practical Guidelines for the Twentieth-Century Single Parent

The Scriptures make it clear, then, that it is possible to be a successful single parent—whether you have to face the *total task* without a marital partner, or whether you have to face the *spiritual* responsibility without the assistance of your unsaved mate. But remember, as a Christian, you need not face the task alone. First of all, you have Jesus Christ in your life. He will never leave you nor forsake you. And second, you are a member of the body of Christ. You are related to other Christians who can and should help you bear your burdens.

Don't get caught in a guilt-trap. Many single parents are bombarded with guilt feelings because of their past lives. True, you may have contributed to a divorce. Let's face it; there probably isn't such a thing as an "innocent party." In our humanness, we all fail.

But remember, Jesus Christ died to save us from our sins. His blood was shed to wash us clean. And "if we confess our sins, He is faithful and just and will forgive us our sins and purify us from *all* unrighteousness" (1 John 1:9).

No matter what your sin, no matter what part you may have had in causing your present situation, Jesus' blood is sufficient to cleanse you. You need not be caught in a guilt-trap. Don't continue to punish yourself for your sins. Jesus has already taken the punishment for you. And don't allow guilt to keep you from doing everything you can to correct the mistakes of the past. You are free! Believe it and begin to act on what *is* a reality.

Don't feel sorry for yourself. Sure, life seems pretty difficult for you as a single parent. The demands may sometimes be almost unbearable. Life may seem impossible. But feeling sorry for yourself will only make your problems worse. Some people burn up tons of energy just dwelling on their problems, when they ought to exert that energy *solving* their problems.

Overcome any anger and bitterness. Persistent feelings of resentment and hostility are devastating to the human personality. And they spill over and touch everyone that is close to you—especially your children. They also interfere with those who want to help you the most. And, furthermore, they also burn up a lot of physical and psychological energy—energy you need to succeed in life.

Forget the past! Concentrate on the present and the future. Thank God you know Christ, that you have forgiveness of sins, that you are a member of the body of Christ. Don't allow your negative emotions to take over and destroy what can be a new beginning.

Here is a practical suggestion to overcome bitterness. Get your mind off yourself. Think about others. Think about the forgiveness you have in Christ. And, if possible, avoid situations that trigger old memories.

Don't expect others to owe you a living. Sure, it's tough. And it may get worse. But don't expect the world or the church to solve your problems. All of us are responsible for our predicaments. True, we may have been a victim of circumstances, but this does not entitle us to simple solutions.

On the other hand, just because you're a Christian, don't let others push you around. Stand up and be counted. Take what is coming to you. For example, I know some Christian divorcees who have allowed their former husbands to take advantage of them, to get by without paying child support, to renege on other agreements. If this kind of behavior persists, report it to your lawyer immediately.

And note! You can do this with a Christian attitude. You need not take revenge or take the law into your own hands. This Paul warns against (see Rom. 12:17-19). But you are entitled to protection *by* the law! Don't bypass your rights in these areas.

Order your life according to biblical priorities. You will need to settle for limited objectives. Most people do, but this is especially true for a single parent. But always operate according to biblical priorities.

Remember that God must be first in your life! Don't neglect your relationship with Him. Read your

Bible and pray. Don't neglect fellowshipping with other Christians and gaining strength from the body of Christ.

Your children come next. Order your life-style so as to do your best to meet their needs—physically, psychologically, and spiritually. True, you won't be able to do everything for them you would like. But remember, a little love that is consistent can go a long, long way.

Don't remarry just for security. Some single parents jump from the frying pan into the fire. They break up with one irresponsible mate and soon find themselves married to another. In the midst of their loneliness and depression and frustration, they become vulnerable. They make a decision that's emotional rather than rational. And lo and behold, they're back where they started, and they're headed for another marital catastrophe. I've known some Christians who even end up marrying a non-Christian, which compounds their problems no end.

Remember! People who have trouble getting along with others are often attracted to people who *also* have difficulty getting along with others. This is not a sound basis for a good marriage. Better to remain single than to end up with another unhappy marriage.

Some Practical Guidelines for the Body of Christ

How can all members of a local body of believers minister to single parents and their children?

Be aware of their presence and their problems. Remember that single parents are members of Christ's body. They, of all people, need love, acceptance, and encouragement.

Avoid having judgmental attitudes. But for God's grace, every one of us could be in their situation. We, too, could be single parents—widowed, separated, divorced. None of us is exempt from human tragedy, from human failure, from serious mistakes. True, some people have gotten themselves into serious predicaments because of their own irresponsible actions, but it's only by God's grace that all of us have not made the same mistakes.

Reach out to the children of single parents. Children of single parents need contact with *both* a father and mother. Even minimal contact helps.

Several years ago, I was counseling a young couple. They were having serious marital problems. Humanly speaking, there was nothing that could be done to hold the marriage together. The young husband and father wanted out, and no effort on my part or anybody's could change his mind. He was in total rebellion against God.

The young woman was left with a beautiful one-year-old daughter. She continued to bring her to church regularly, and I made a special effort every week to make contact with this little girl—to hold her, to talk to her, just to love her. My efforts, of course, were limited. But in a simple way I was helping to provide this little girl with a father substitute.

No one individual, of course, can minister to *all* the children who need substitute fathers and mothers. But if every member of Christ's body would make it a point to reach out to just one child, there would be unbelievable results in the lives of these children—and their parents.

Let me suggest a practical project. First, make sure

your nursery and Sunday School are staffed with both men and women. This in itself will enable children from single-parent homes to have contact with both father and mother substitutes.

Second, have every single parent in your church who desires to have someone take a special interest in their children indicate this desire in some specific way—for example, by filling out a special form. Then have every member of the body of Christ who would like to minister to a child of a single parent also indicate this interest on a similar form. Then match up these people with at least one child.

A word of caution! Single parents should not set their expectation levels too high, nor should other members of the body set their goals too high. Personal contact may have to be minimal. Remember that most parents don't spend enough time with their own children. We must not neglect our own while ministering to others.

Another word of caution. It is a good idea for both fathers and mothers to relate to a child of a single parent. Emotions run high in these relationships. For example, a single mother may respond emotionally to *any* man who reaches out to her child. Just be on guard! Don't let a good thing turn into a tragedy.

Family Project

As a family, think of and pray about adopting another family who has only one parent. Your goal would be to pray for that family regularly, to invite them to your home periodically, and to plan other special events with them.

11 DIVORCE AND REMARRIAGE
A BIBLICAL VIEWPOINT

With every passing year, the number of divorces compared with marriages increases proportionately. For example, in 1940, there was one divorce for every six marriages. Twenty years later, in 1960, the number increased to one in every four. By 1970 it was almost one in every three. If this trend continues—and there appears to be nothing that will reverse it—think what it will be like in 1980! Or by 1990! Some predict there will very soon be one divorce for every marriage.

As Christians, we must realize that what transpires

in our culture *generally* certainly affects Christians *particularly*. And what is happening in the realm of marriage is no exception. Many Christian couples are also being plagued with marital unhappiness—and eventual divorce. Ask any Christian counselor.

Furthermore, many people are becoming Christians who have already suffered through divorce proceedings. In some sections of the country, scores of divorcees are becoming members of the Christian family through a personal relationship with Jesus Christ. In fact, the traumatic experience of divorce often causes people to reach out to God. In their despair and searching, they discover a new Friend— Jesus Christ—who will never leave them nor forsake them.

But how would you counsel the Christian couple seeking a divorce? There are Christians who want to be released from marriage. There are Christians who feel that they don't love their mates any more. There are Christians who are attracted to other persons and would rather be with those persons than with their own marital partners. There are Christian married couples whose relationships are cold and unsatisfying. How would you counsel them? What would you say? And, more particularly, what should be your attitude if you happen to be one of the persons described?

For ultimate answers, we can only turn to one basic source—the Bible. All else will lead us astray. The value systems in our society offer only man's solutions—not God's! Non-Christian counselors are legion, but so are their opinions. The Bible gives God's viewpoint. But what is it?

A Biblical Viewpoint

The Bible is our *only* reliable source for discovering God's specific perspective on divorce and remarriage. Unfortunately, not all evangelical scholars agree regarding what the Bible really teaches. In fact, some of my most respected friends, fellow professors, and pastors hold opposite points of view. And this leads us to what I personally believe is a rather safe conclusion—wherever you have respected Christian scholars who agree that the Bible is indeed God's Word, but who disagree about what it teaches, you can be quite sure that the subject is not totally clear in Scripture. If it were, there would be a consensus—as there is on such subjects as how to become a Christian, the deity of Jesus Christ, the death, resurrection, and ascension of Christ, and the Second Coming. But there is no such consensus among Bible-believing Christians about divorce and remarriage.

It seems to me that this observation leads to yet another conclusion. When dealing with a biblical subject where Christian scholars disagree, we must be careful to be certain and dogmatic *only* when the Bible is very clear, and cautious and tentative when it is not. This is difficult to do, for all of us want clear-cut, biblical answers, especially if we are loyal to God's Word. Unfortunately, however, many of us have a low tolerance for ambiguity, and we get very frustrated if everything is not black and white.

Well, I must warn you in advance! This chapter will probably not answer *all* of your questions—or mine. And the reason is obvious. The Bible really doesn't give us *all* the answers, at least in relationship to specific problems in the twentieth century.

Having said this, let me now hurry to add that the Bible *does* speak clearly about certain aspects of marriage, divorce, and even remarriage. Let's look at these certainties first.

Divorce is not within God's ideal plan. It goes without saying that death of one partner dissolves a marriage union and sets the Christian free to marry again. Here the Scriptures are very clear (see Rom. 7:1-4; 1 Cor. 7:8,9; 1 Tim. 5:14). But the Bible also makes it clear from the very beginning when God first created man and woman and brought them together as husband and wife that He wanted them to stay together until they were separated by death. Thus we read— "For this cause a man shall leave his father and his mother, and shall cleave to his wife; and they shall become one flesh" (Gen. 2:24).

The word "cleave" is a very strong word. It implies permanence in the marriage relationship. And Jesus Christ, in referring to the same Scripture, left no doubts about what God had in mind for every couple who enters the holy state of marriage—"They are no longer two, but one," said Jesus. "Therefore what God has joined together, *let man not separate*" (Matt. 19:6).

Divorce, then, is not within God's ideal plan and His perfect will. And He could not be clearer about this issue than when He said to Israel—"Let no one deal treacherously against the wife of your youth. 'For I hate divorce,' says the Lord, the God of Israel" (Mal. 2:15,16).

Sin interfered with God's ideal plan. Sin affected God's ideal plan for mankind, including marital harmony and happiness. Though God's perfect will did not include divorce and remarriage, He allowed it because of the presence of sin in the world.

Though nowhere in Scripture can we find a *command* to divorce another person, we can find references that directly teach that God permitted it under certain circumstances. The clearest passage is in Deuteronomy 24:1, which refers to a "certificate of divorce" being issued because of "indecency"—although we don't know what the indecency was. And it is also clear from this passage that both parties were permitted to remarry (24:2,3).

This biblical reality, though clear, poses some problems for Christians today. Though it is obvious from Scripture that God tolerated divorce and remarriage, the illustrations and examples in Scripture are very limited, and those that are included do not give us sufficient information to understand all of the particulars.

We've already noted one example of this. In Deuteronomy 24, we do not even know for sure what kind of "indecency" was involved. We do know that it was probably not adultery because the penalty for this sin in the Old Testament was death and nothing is said here about that penalty (see Lev. 20:10; Deut. 22:22). And furthermore, the illustration in Deuteronomy only involves the sin of the woman. What about men? Are they excluded? Not according to Jesus, as we'll see later (see John 8:1-11; Mark 10:11,12).

But note something very important. Because we *do* have sinful natures, our tendency is to misuse information that is not totally clear in Scripture, and to abuse biblical silence. This the Pharisees did continually. Some interpreted this Deuteronomy passage in ridiculous ways, primarily to indulge sinful and selfish natures. This is the setting for the questions they asked Jesus. And their motive was obvious. They were trying to "test" Jesus. Consequently, they asked, "Is it lawful for a man to divorce his wife for *any* and *every* reason?" (Matt. 19:3).

To understand this question, you must understand that some Jewish leaders came up with unbelievable interpretations of this Old Testament passage in Deuteronomy 24. For example, the following comes from the extra-biblical Jewish laws, giving reasons why a man could divorce his wife—"If she ... does not set aside a dough-offering, or utters a vow and does not fulfill it .... If she goes out with her hair unbound, or spins in the street, or speaks with any man .... Also (if she is) a scolding woman. And who is a scolding woman? Whoever speaks inside her house so that her neighbors hear her voice."[1]

If these statements really represented God's will, it would give nearly every person grounds for divorce. It is a pathetic picture of what man's sinful nature will do—under the guise of biblical teaching. Jesus made it clear that this is not what God had in mind. In fact, He went back to the beginning of marriage—as it was instituted in the Garden of Eden.

" 'Haven't you read,' he replied, 'that at the beginning the Creator "made them male and female," and said, "For this reason a man will leave his father and mother and be united to his wife, and the two will become one flesh"? So they are no longer two, but one. Therefore what God has joined together, let man not separate.'

162

" 'Why then,' they asked, 'did Moses *command* that a man give his wife a certificate of divorce and send her away?'

"Jesus replied, 'Moses *permitted* you to divorce your wives because your hearts were hard. But it was not this way from the beginning. I tell you that anyone who divorces his wife, except for marital unfaithfulness, and marries another woman commits adultery' " (Matt. 19:4-9).

A careful study of Deuteronomy 24:1-4 indicates that no *command* is involved (see the *NASB* translation) and Jesus corrected this false interpretation of Moses when He replied—"Moses *permitted* you to divorce your wives because your hearts were hard."

But we must also note that even Jesus' answer to the Pharisees does not settle all of our problems nor answer all of our questions. In fact, it is not totally clear what Jesus meant by "marital unfaithfulness" as a justification for divorce. Various interpretations are given by equally competent scholars. (The Greek word *porneia* which is translated "marital unfaithfulness" in the *New International Version* and "fornication" in the *King James Version*, refers to a variety of illegitimate sexual acts and behavior. See, for example, 1 Cor. 5:1 where the word is translated incest, and Acts 15:20, 29, where it probably refers to Jewish rules regarding the relationships between sexes, or particular laws for Jewish men and women regarding sex.)

Does the lack of complete agreement among scholars mean we cannot trust the Bible? No. It only means that for some reason God has not given us all the answers regarding divorce and remarriage. We do know, though, for sure, that God's *perfect* will from the beginning did not include divorce and remarriage, apart from death of one marital partner, but we also know for sure that because of sin in the world, He allowed it. And one reason He allowed it was that marriage involves two people. When Adam and Eve sinned in the garden, they were *each* held responsible. But when two people marry, one person may be more at fault than the other, causing the marriage to disintegrate.

Putting it another way, when it comes to sin *generally*, each of us is judged *specifically*. Each of us is held responsible for personal actions. But in marriage, one partner may be involved more specifically in sin than the other, leading to a very difficult situation for the partner who really wants the marriage to work. Consequently, as we'll see more clearly later, if a partner does all he or she can to keep the relationship together, but cannot, it appears that he or she is permitted by God to participate in a divorce without being condemned.

The blood of Christ can atone for all sin. A third certainty from Scripture is that no sin is so great that it cannot be forgiven—including adultery and unjustified divorce and remarriage. Nothing could be clearer in Scripture. Listen to Paul as he wrote to the Corinthians—"Do not be deceived: Neither the sexually immoral nor idolaters nor adulterers nor male prostitutes nor homosexual offenders nor thieves nor the greedy nor drunkards nor slanderers nor swindlers will inherit the kingdom of God. And that is what *some of you were*. But you were *washed*, you were *sanctified*, you were justified in the name of the

164

Lord Jesus Christ and by the Spirit of our God" (1 Cor. 6:9-11).

The apostle John confirmed this when he wrote, "If we confess our sins, he is faithful and just and will forgive us our sins and purify us from *all* unrighteousness" (1 John 1:9). Though there may be lack of clarity surrounding some of the specific aspects of divorce and remarriage, there are no such question marks surrounding the concept of forgiveness. The blood of Christ is sufficient to cleanse a person from *every* sin he can ever commit. Any other view of the atonement sets limits on the cleansing power of the blood of Christ.

Some of us as Christians have become guilty of putting "marriage sins" in a special class that cannot be forgiven. This we cannot do and be consistent with Scripture. No sin is too great to be forgiven. King David illustrates this graphically—even under the Old Testament Law. He committed both adultery and murder. According to the Law, he should have been executed for his sins (see Lev. 20:10). But he wasn't! He confessed his sin, demonstrated true sorrow, and pleaded for God's mercy. God forgave him.

Jesus, who Himself was the very *means* of forgiveness, set the extreme example for forgiveness. When a group of pious scribes and Pharisees brought a woman taken in the act of adultery, quoting the law that she should die, Jesus responded, "He who is without sin among you, let him be the first to throw a stone at her" (John 8:7). While He was saying this, He was writing in the sand with His finger. One by one, each man walked away, leaving the woman alone with Jesus.

I've often wondered what Jesus wrote. It might have been the number of times each man had committed adultery—and perhaps with whom. Whatever He wrote, they got the message clearly. They were as guilty as she was and they had no right to take her life. Christ's response to this woman, as she stood alone with Him, leaves no room for speculation regarding the possibility of forgiveness. Listen to John's account—"Jesus straightened up and asked her, 'Woman, where are they? Has no one condemned you?'

" 'No one, sir,' she said.

" 'Then neither do I condemn you,' Jesus declared. 'Go now and leave your life of sin.' "

We see, then, that even in the Old Testament, and especially in the New, there was a higher law than the law of condemnation. It is the law of forgiveness, which takes effect when we truly turn to God in repentance, confessing our sins, accepting forgiveness through the ultimate sacrifice of Jesus Christ.

But at this point we must add a fourth certainty in Scripture that relates directly to the subject of divorce and remarriage. We don't like to acknowledge it, but it's true nevertheless.

Sin results in suffering. When we are involved in a situation that is out of harmony with God's perfect plan, we usually suffer the natural consequences. We cannot sin against God and get away with it. God's ideal is permanence for marriage. When we violate that reality, we will suffer from the natural results, some more than others, depending on individual situations.

Unfortunately, even those who are not primarily at

fault will also suffer the consequences of our sin. This was certainly true in David's life. Though he was forgiven, his heart was broken because of the sins of his own children, who unfortunately followed his bad example. Furthermore, God had told Israel that He would visit the iniquity of the fathers on the children, on the third and fourth generations (see Exod. 20:5).

We cannot violate God's ideals without affecting other people—especially those closest to us. Being responsible for a divorce will not only affect the one responsible, but others who may not be primarily responsible. Frequently, the children get the worst end of the deal.

We can conclude, then, that there are at least four major certainties in Scripture relative to divorce. First, it is not a part of God's ideal plan. Second, because of the principle of sin which is operative in the world, affecting all human relationships, God permits divorce and remarriage. Third, God has made provision for the forgiveness of our sins—no matter what they are. But fourth, He does not guarantee total disentanglement from the natural consequences and effects of that sin.

Solving Today's Problems

We must, it seems, approach the problems of divorce and remarriage in the twentieth century on the basis and in the light of these four major biblical certainties. Against the backdrop of these theological realities, we can then use the specific, but limited, illustrations and teachings of Scripture to help us answer specific contemporary questions. These four absolutes will help us interpret and apply what is meant by the various biblical examples, even though God did not reveal to us all the specific details. In fact, without these broad biblical guidelines, it may appear that the various divorce and remarriage incidents in Scripture are contradictory in some respects. But when we look at them in the light of these four certainties, we see harmony and consistency.

The following questions and answers, then, represent my own personal approach to specific situations. At this point I feel I must be tentative and cautious rather than dogmatic.

What if marriage problems occur before a person becomes a Christian?

Here we must take seriously the law of forgiveness. God blots out the past as far as condemnation is concerned. From His perspective, we can begin a new life. This doesn't mean, however, that we may not have to face the *results* of our sin. The consequences of divorce vary, depending upon the many variables involved. The results depend to a great extent on whether or not there are children involved. Another result of sin is the inability to blot out memories of the past. Human beings, constructed as they are, will always compare one emotional experience with another. This often leads to psychological confusion and unhappiness. But natural consequences do not usually rule out the opportunity to start over and, in many instances, to find emotional healing.

What if one mate is unfaithful to the other?

Again, we must look at God's perfect will. His desire is that a marriage relationship not be severed by man—although it can happen. Otherwise Jesus would not have said—"Let man not separate." If a marriage could not be broken, He would probably have said—"What God has joined together, *man can never separate.*" But He didn't.

However, even though humans can sever a marriage relationship, they should do everything possible to save a marriage. Scripture is clear. We should forgive those who have sinned against us, including a marriage partner.

But God is aware that some situations are impossible. This is why He tolerated divorce. There may be no repentance on the part of the one involved in sexual immorality. Humanly speaking, there seems to be no way to save this kind of marriage. Under these circumstances, God allowed divorce without condemnation of the one who had made every effort to restore harmony. This appears to be the meaning of Christ's words in Matthew 5:32 and 19:9.

God allows divorce when there has been "marital unfaithfulness" in the sphere of sexual intimacy. And to be consistent with the spirit of Scripture and the words of Jesus, we must conclude that this would include constant, persistent, and flagrant mental adultery. Jesus said, "I tell you that anyone who looks at a woman lustfully has already committed adultery with her in his heart" (Matt. 5:28).

Under these circumstances, can the mate who has been faithful remarry?

It appears that he or she can. The implication from Scripture appears to be that divorce under these circumstances dissolves the marriage relationship and sets the person free to marry again.

What if there has been no sexual unfaithfulness in a Christian marriage, but two Christians decide to

169

leave each other because of incompatibility?

This appears to be the question Paul was answering in 1 Corinthians 7:10,11—"To the married, I give this command (not I, but the Lord): A wife must not separate from her husband. But if she does, she must remain unmarried or else be reconciled to her husband. And a husband must not divorce his wife."

In other words, if we can project the actual question that the Corinthians were asking Paul (see 1 Cor. 7:1), he was responding by saying that two *Christians* should work out their problems. To divorce for any grounds other than sexual immorality is not acceptable to God. And to marry someone else under these conditions is doubly wrong. They should seek to be reconciled to each other. However, if they cannot be reconciled, Paul seems to give permission to remain apart, but not to get remarried.

What if one Christian partner tries to reconcile, but the other will not respond? Is remarriage ever justified?

If the person who refuses to reconcile marries someone else, the moment that happens he or she has been involved in marital unfaithfulness. In this case, and on the basis of other biblical illustrations, it appears that the other party is now free to remarry.

But there is yet another perspective involving a procedure spelled out by Jesus Christ. He was dealing with a problem where one Christian had sinned against another. This is what He said: "If your brother sins against you, go and show him his fault, just between the two of you. If he listens to you, you have won your brother over. But if he will not listen, take one or two others along, so that 'every matter may be established by the testimony of two or three witnesses.' If he refuses to listen to them, tell it to the church; and if he refuses to listen even to the church, treat him as you would a pagan or a tax collector" (Matt. 18:15-17).

Applying this Scripture directly to a marriage relationship involving two Christians, as I believe we can, Jesus is saying that a Christian partner who does not respond to God's will when properly confronted in love should be viewed as a non-Christian. If this be true, Paul's statement in 1 Corinthians about *an unbelieving* partner would apply too. But this leads us to our next question which involves a Christian who is married to a non-Christian.

What if a Christian is married to an unbeliever who wants a divorce?

First, a Christian mate should do everything possible to win the respect and love of the unsaved person, with the hope that he or she might come to know Jesus Christ personally. This is specifically pointed out by the apostle Peter in his first epistle (see 1 Pet. 3:1-7). Paul also speaks to this issue in his Corinthian epistle, giving more detail to help us know what to do if the unbeliever does not respond to the Christian mate's efforts.

Paul wrote: "To the rest I say this (I, not the Lord): If any brother has a wife who is not a believer and she is willing to live with him, he must not divorce her. And if a woman has a husband who is not a believer and he is willing to live with her, she must not divorce him. For the unbelieving husband has been sanctified through his wife, and the unbelieving wife has been sanctified through her believing husband. Otherwise, your children would be 'unclean,' but as it is, they are holy. But if the unbeliever leaves, let him do so. A believing man or woman is not bound in such circumstances; God has called us to live in peace" (1 Cor. 7:12-15).[2]

It appears, then, from these verses, that the Christian mate is free to remarry if the non-Christian mate leaves and will not be reconciled. As Paul said, "A believing man or woman is not bound in such circumstances" (1 Cor. 7:15). The overall thrust of the Bible seems to support the conclusion that by no longer being *bound* implies *freedom* to remarry. But obviously only to a Christian.

Going back then to the previous question, it appears that if a believing mate does not respond to church discipline as spelled out by Jesus Christ, the believing mate who wants reconciliation can now view the uncooperative partner as a non-Christian. This would free the believing partner to divorce and remarry. Paul's words appear to apply in this case— "A believing man or woman is not bound in such circumstances." But this action may be taken only after every effort has been made according to biblical procedures to restore the one who is resisting the will of God.

What if a Christian has violated all of God's commands regarding marriage, but now is a devoted Christian? Can a person ever remarry under these circumstances?

There appears to be only one major truth to bring to bear upon this question—God's forgiveness. There is no sin, it seems, that His blood will not cover, including marital sins. To be consistent with Scripture, we must put marital sins in the same category as premarital sins. No Christian who knows the Bible can deny that God forgives premarital sins. When an unmarried Christian or a non-Christian joins himself to another person sexually and becomes one with that person (see 1 Cor. 6:16), he certainly can experience forgiveness. Very few would try to prove from Scripture that the person so involved could not get married because of his premarital unchastity. How then can we insist that God will not forgive *marital* sins of the same nature?

Even in these cases, however, we must recognize that we "reap what we sow." Premarital sins, as well as marital sins, though forgiven by Jesus Christ, often create adjustment problems in marriage. Whenever we violate God's laws, we must suffer the natural consequences—even though our sins are forgiven.

Can a person who has been divorced and remarried ever effectively serve Jesus Christ as a spiritual leader in the church?

I believe a person can. Some Christians argue that the qualification for eldership in 1 Timothy 3:2 and Titus 1:6 to be the "husband of one wife" refers to divorce and remarriage. I do not believe it does. The Greek words simply mean "a one-woman man" or "a one-wife man," and this grammatical ambiguity demands a much broader biblical and cultural perspective to determine what Paul really meant.

I believe that Paul was demanding that a man who is chosen for spiritual leadership in his church was to be loyal to his wife and to her alone. For example, he was to give up his contacts with any girls in the pagan temples—which men in the first century often maintained as regular sexual companions.

Having said this, I must add that a person chosen for any spiritual leadership position in his church must be chosen on the basis of *all* the qualities listed in 1 Timothy 3 and Titus 1. And, especially, if divorced and remarried, he must have a good reputation among both Christians and non-Christians, and have his household in good order. Usually a man who has more than one household will not have things in good order. In other words, a man who has been divorced and remarried is often disqualified from spiritual leadership, not because of his present marital status, but because of the absence of other spiritual qualifications. This is why a man must be chosen on the basis of *all* the spiritual qualities. But if a man who is divorced and remarried meets all of the other qualifications, I personally could not oppose his appointment as an elder in the church on the basis of Paul's statement—"the husband of one wife."

Here I believe we must consider the apostle Paul as a dynamic example. Many of us do not stop to consider the fact that as a non-Christian he was a murderer. He killed Christians because they did not agree with his Jewish theology. And murder was a violation of God's law—even though Paul thought he was justified according to his interpretation of the law. But when he confessed his sins and became a Christian, God forgave him and called him to be the great apostle to the Gentiles. And God also used him to pen more New Testament books than any other first-century Christian.

In view of the whole panorama of Scripture and its emphasis on forgiveness, I cannot put divorce and remarriage in a category that is more restrictive than murder. That attitude does not seem to correlate with God's nature and actions.

But a divorced person who is serving Jesus Christ must never flaunt the grace of God. Neither must he or she ever give others the impression that a marriage should not be permanent. In fact, it is probably wise for divorced people who are in leadership roles to avoid discussing their situation publicly. It only gives Satan an opportunity to cause confusion; one of his tricks is to cause other people to rationalize future action in their own lives.

Practical Guidelines for Remarriage

If you feel you have biblical grounds for remarriage, consider the following additional guidelines to help you in your decision.

1. Is it impossible to reconcile with my mate? Have I done everything I can to bring this about?

(If your previous mate is remarried, obviously this will be impossible.)

2. Is my relationship with Jesus Christ what it should be? Do I have it together spiritually?

This is your first priority. I would never advise remarriage for any person who has not first tested and proved his or her love and commitment to Jesus Christ. If you are not committed to Him and consistent in your Christian walk, you will have real difficulty in another marriage. Be sure to prove your commitment to yourself and others over a substantial period of time.

3. Do I have it together psychologically?

Ask other people you trust to give you their frank

175

opinion. If you're emotionally immature—a major reason contributing to many divorces—you'll need to solve that problem first.

Note: The following are symptoms that need to be dealt with and solved before you consider remarriage —bitterness, anger, depression, lack of self-discipline, and sexual problems. If you had difficulty functioning sexually in your first marriage because of psychological hang-ups or physical problems, chances are you'll have difficulty in your second. Under these circumstances, and while these conditions exist, it is advisable not to remarry. Marriage for security alone may quickly lead to another divorce.

4. Am I psychologically capable of handling another marriage?

If you have been divorced—and especially more than once—you may be incapable psychologically of handling the demands of a marriage. It is probably wise for you to remain unmarried, at least for a lengthy period of time until you have demonstrated to yourself and everyone else that you are emotionally mature.

5. Am I personally inadequate? Is this my motive for remarriage?

Some divorced people try desperately to find happiness in a relationship with the opposite sex because of their personal inadequacies. They are not capable of *giving*—they only want to *receive*. If you are that kind of person, you would be foolish to consider another marriage. Until you solve that problem, the chances are great that you'd be heading for another marital catastrophe.

6. How well do I understand my personality?

Before considering remarriage, seek counsel from a competent Christian counselor or psychologist who will be honest with you. Also be honest with him. Request a battery of tests that will really reveal the level of your psychological maturity.

7. *Is the person I am considering remarrying also a divorcee?*

Be cautious in marrying another divorced person. If his or her problems happen to be the same as yours, you will compound the possibilities of entering another marriage that may not work. A second divorce is definitely devastating and may make it more difficult to cope with life.

A Family or Group Project

Using the guidelines in this chapter, discuss how you would counsel a married couple seeking a divorce.

Footnotes

1. *Mishnah*, translated by Danby, p. 255.
2. Again, scholars disagree as to what Paul had in mind when he said, "Not the Lord." I cannot accept this as meaning that Paul is merely giving his own idea. I believe that he was speaking inspired truth, but that he had no knowledge that Christ ever spoke about this issue while on earth.

12 MOVING
FROM FUNCTION
TO FORM

Edith Schaeffer, in her book on the home, describes the family as a mobile. She writes: "A family is the most versatile, ever-changing mobile that exists. The family is a *living* mobile that is different from the hand-craft mobiles and the art-museum mobiles, different from the mobiles of lakes and trees, from the mobiles of birds, fish, and animals—different from any mobile of machine, animal, or plant. A family is an intricate mobile made up of human personalities."[1]

Though analogies are always limited in explaining some truth, this is one of the best I've heard describing the Christian family. A mobile is always dynamic —*moving* and *changing*. There is never a moment when it is totally static.

This is certainly true of the family. It begins with a husband and wife, whose personalities and total makeup both add the potential for infinite creativity and variety in a family. God's plan is that children be added to this union—each one different, each one with his or her own set of problems and potentialities. As hour follows hour, day follows day, and week follows week, every person in a family is changing. The changes of one affect all others. There is constant change. No form or pattern is ever sufficient to solve all problems.

Yes, it is true. People are born to function. Wherever you have function you have form. What usually distinguishes a Christian family from a non-Christian family are the *functions* described in the Bible, and the principles and goals which make the Christian family unique. These functions and principles and goals help us to design forms and structures that will enable us to be a New Testament family living in the twentieth century.

Biblical Goals, Functions, and Principles

This book has described biblical functions, goals, and principles for daily Christian living. In order to have a proper final perspective, let's review—but with a specific purpose in mind.

A basic guideline for any marriage. When describing the family from a Christian point of view, one very important truth emerges. To have a truly Christian family that is functioning properly, both partners must be dedicated Christians. This, of course, is obvious. But many people seem to forget this important guideline when considering marriage—or even when trying to analyze what has gone wrong with their marriage.

Paul made this point clear in his second letter to the Corinthians—"Do not be yoked together with unbelievers" (2 Cor. 6:14). And though Paul had in mind relationships in general, he certainly included the most intimate relationship of all—marriage.

There are situations, of course, that emerge during life's journey that create problems. For example, after marriage one mate may become a Christian while the other does not. Furthermore, marrying a Christian doesn't guarantee a happy marriage, for it takes two committed and spiritual Christians to achieve God's ideal in marriage. At any given time, one Christian may choose to live a sinful and selfish life. Obviously, this will interfere with God's plan.

The Bible acknowledges these realities and, as we've seen, provides guidelines for people with these problems. But to be forewarned is to be forearmed. If you are a Christian, marry a Christian. And more than that, marry a mature Christian. This assumes that you must also be a mature Christian.

An awesome reality. There is a reality in Scripture I could wish were not there. But it is true. And it cannot be changed, because it is God's law. And it is verified again and again in human experience. We suffer the natural consequences of our sins.

My appeal here is primarily to young people who have their lives ahead of them. When it comes to relationships with the opposite sex, keep yourself pure. Avoid emotional and physical entanglement that could create frustration, anxiety, resentment, and guilt. Wait until that time, that moment in marriage, when God will smile on all you do and you will be totally free with each other as God intended.

Don't spoil now what God intended to be beautiful and free from all kinds of emotional hang-ups.

Several years ago, I participated in a national survey of 3,000 Christian teenagers. In one section of the questionnaire, the young people were asked to indicate on a four-point scale the extent to which each of 40 goals occupied their thinking—*never, a little, some,* or *much.* One of these goals was "making a happy marriage." Over 70 percent responded by saying they think about this goal "much."

Unfortunately, many young people do not realize that by violating God's basic laws of moral purity they are interfering with the very thing they so much want.

Three spiritual goals. There are three basic goals for a Christian family—as there are for the church. First, a family of Christians should reflect *faith* in God. Believe what He says, and act on that faith. Don't put your trust in material things. "But seek first his kingdom and his righteousness, and all these things will be given to you as well" (Matt. 6:33).

Second, develop *hope.* Be doctrinally stable as a family. Know what you believe, and believe what you know. Become a family that loves and lives the Bible.

Third, and most important, be a *loving* community. Care for each other. This is the hallmark of Christian maturity, and the one that God will use the most to minister to others. For it is these three ingredients—faith, hope, and love—but especially love —that lead to unity and oneness and will enable you as a family to be a dynamic witness to the larger community where you live.

Four distinctive functions. There are four major

functions described in the Bible that set a Christian family off from the secular and non-Christian family. We looked at these functions extensively in previous chapters. They are submission, headship with love, obedience to parents, and Christian nurture of children.

But note! These are *functions*. The Bible does not describe specifically what forms these functions should take, although it gives us unique guidelines and principles. The chart on pages 184, 185 will help summarize what the Scriptures teach about these functions and will in turn set the stage for helping us to develop proper forms and structures.

Christians often make two basic mistakes regarding form and structure. First, because the Bible says little about it, we sometimes try to function without it. This is impossible. You cannot have function without form, organism without organization. To try to do without form leads to chaos, confusion, and ineffectiveness—both in the church and in the home.

Another serious mistake is to superimpose form upon biblical function, either in the church or in the home. At the church level, we often equate certain cultural behavior with required biblical behavior—such as when we meet, what people wear, where people should sit, how the service is structured, how many times a week we meet, who can speak. In the family, we can do the same thing if we're not careful. For example, let's look at some examples where we sometimes lock ourselves into areas where we should be free.

Submission and headship. Some Christians believe that the concept of submission and headship means

A BIBLICAL PROFILE ON THE FAMILY

Basic Goals and Guidelines

1. Before marriage, make sure you are spiritually and psychologically mature (see Rom. 12:1,2).

2. Approach marriage as being a permanent relationship. This is God's perfect will (see Matt. 19:4-6).

3. Marry only a Christian who is also spiritually and psychologically mature (see 2 Cor. 6:14).

4. Avoid behavior in your unmarried life that will cause you to have hang-ups in your married life.

Functions and Principles

1. **Function:** wifely submission (see Eph. 5:22,23)

   Principles:
   a. obedience
   b. a gentle and quiet spirit
   c. commitment, dedication, and love
   d. making the home a priority

2. **Function:** headship with love (see Eph. 5:25-33; 1 Pet. 3:7)

   Principles:
   a. unselfishness
   b. humility and servanthood

Basic Forms and Patterns

Here the Bible sets us free and does not lock us into predetermined patterns and structures. We are responsible to develop appropriate forms that will help us reach biblical goals and carry out scriptural functions.

c. self-sacrifice

d. understanding and sensitivity

3. **Function:** childhood obedience (see Eph. 6:1-3).

   Principles:
   a. respect
   b. honor

4. **Function:** parental nurture (see Eph. 6:4)

   Principles: (see Deut. 6:6-9; Prov. 22:6):
   a. a proper father image
   b. a constant example
   c. spontaneity
   d. discipline: love and patience; insight into age levels and the natural bent

5. Set three basic spiritual goals for your family—corporate faith, corporate hope, and corporate love (see 1 Cor. 13:13).

6. Remember that all believers have a sin nature that will make living according to God's ideal a constant challenge; but remember, too, that God has provided the means to overcome the effects of the old nature if we desire to be obedient to His Word (see 1 Cor. 10:13).

Note: Form and good organization are very important in the family. If they are lacking, it can lead to all kinds of misunderstandings, insecurity, and insensitivity. The important principle is that we must not get locked into patterns, but be willing to change and be flexible when necessary.

185

that a woman should never work outside the home. Or they believe that it means that a woman should never be trusted with the bank account and never be involved with business affairs and decisions. These may be acceptable forms to some couples, but they are not forms we find in the Bible. It is possible to practice submission and headship without this approach to marriage and family life.

Some men are perfectly happy to have their wives work and be involved totally in the operation of the family. The man is still the head of the household and the wife is submissive to her husband. There is no violation of biblical principles if the wife can be involved in this way without neglecting her husband and family. They are simply using a different form to carry out biblical function.

On the other hand, I know wives who are very happy to be completely uninvolved in the financial matters of the family. They like living on an allowance and they never would want to work. They prefer it that way. If so, this is a freedom established in Scripture. The important point is that no matter what our forms and structures for family function, they must never violate biblical principles.

Sexual function. This is a very important part of marriage. In fact, it is commanded. But in this area God also allows a great deal of freedom. God's laws include one man and one woman. This is the absolute. But it does not set restrictions on sexual behavior within marriage, particularly if it does not violate the principles of sensitivity, understanding, and unselfishness. The very nature of our sexual makeup provides a man and woman with unusual potential for creativity. And yet, some Christians superimpose restrictions on sex within marriage, usually because of cultural hang-ups and misunderstandings. Again, we see freedom in form.

Family nurture. Bringing up our children in the nurture and admonition of the Lord provides us with unusual opportunities for creativity. God does not lock us into a stereotyped approach. In fact, the very nature of a growing and changing family calls for constant variation and change in our approach to nurture and discipline. An approach in discipline that works with one child may not work with another.

We must deal with each child as an individual personality, with individual personal needs. There is no one way to discipline a child. We cannot tell a parent he is right or wrong—unless he is violating the principles and guidelines of Scripture, such as love, understanding, sensitivity, and insight into a child's nature.

Childhood obedience. Even obedience in children takes on different forms and expressions. Various families have their own understanding of what acceptable obedience is. We must not judge parents who differ from us in their approach. A parent has freedom to insist on what he wants, providing he is not violating New Testament principles and guidelines.

It is very important, of course, that we always test our motives in light of biblical guidelines. For example, are our demands unfair? Are they selfish? Are they insensitive? Do they ignore culture? On the other hand, are we ignoring moral values? Are we uninvolved with the child's life, making judgments that are not based on knowledge? Are we overly permissive? And also important, does our approach create an unusual problem for other parents? If it does, we are probably creating problems for our own children because they will have difficulty functioning in the cultural context in which they live. It's important that we be sensitive to other members in Christ's body. This, too, is a biblical principle.

One of the major problems in the world today is that many Christians are traveling here and there, conducting seminars and dispensing forms and patterns in effective child-rearing and other aspects of family living. This often becomes confusing to parents because what may work in one home may not work in another. Furthermore, people try to duplicate the *formulas* without understanding the *principles* underlying them. This is why we must go back to basic goals, principles, and biblical functions, and show parents how to apply these truths creatively in their own cultural situations. This, I believe, represents a biblical approach to communication.

Don't misunderstand. I'm not saying it's wrong to illustrate how to apply these principles. But frequently people do not understand the principles and only hear what we're saying about the way to do it. In other words, the illustrations often overshadow the principles and people miss the basic message.

A Final Word

Yes, the family *is* like a mobile. It is an ever-changing cluster of human personalities that is constantly affecting each other. And as we know, a mobile usually moves with the slightest disturbance.

Here is also a dynamic lesson. Some movement is necessary, good, and normal. In fact, change in form is inevitable. But there are also winds that must be controlled when it comes to the Christian family "mobile." Thus Paul said we must become mature in Christ so we "will no longer be infants, tossed back and forth by the waves, and blown here and there *by every wind of teaching* and by the cunning and craftiness of men in their deceitful scheming" (Eph. 4:14).

James also added: "If any of you lacks wisdom, he should ask God, who gives generously to all without finding fault, and it will be given to him. But when he asks, he must believe and not doubt, because he who doubts is like a wave of the sea, blown and tossed by the *wind*" (Jas. 1:5,6).

Freedom in form, then, must always conform to biblical absolutes. We must hold unswervingly to that which will *never change*, but be open, free, and creative in the areas that are not absolute. We must not change form just to be changing, but neither must we refuse to change because of our own insecurities and confusion. The Christian family presents the greatest challenge ever to maintain a proper balance—especially since most secular families are like a ship at sea, caught in a storm. The rudder is broken and they are unknowingly headed for the reefs. This need not be true of the Christian family no matter how strong the winds, no matter how dangerous the seas.

The Christian family has a guidebook that clearly charts the course, and we have a Pilot who has been this way before. Because He is our "great high priest who has gone into heaven, Jesus the Son of God, let us hold firmly to the faith we profess. For we do not have a high priest who is unable to sympathize with our weaknesses, but we have one who has been tempted in every way, just as we are—yet was without sin. Let us then approach the throne of grace with confidence, so that we may receive mercy and find grace to help us in our time of need" (Heb. 4:14-16).

A Family or Group Project

Review the Life Response at the conclusion of each chapter. How are your attitudes and behavior different now than they were when you first worked through them?

Footnote
1. Edith Schaeffer, *What Is a Family?* (Old Tappan, N.J.: Fleming H. Revell Co., 1975), p. 18.